YES!
YOU CAN
STOP SMOKING
Revised

EVEN IF YOU DON'T WANT TO
By David C. Jones

Dolphin Publishing
West Palm Beach, Florida

I

ACKNOWLEDGMENTS

The Surgeon General's Report on
Nicotine Addiction

American Psychiatric Association's Diagnostic and
Statistical Manual of Mental Disorders, IV

The American Cancer Society

The American Lung Association

The American Heart Association

Nicotine Anonymous World Services
P.O. Box 59177
San Francisco, CA 94159-1777
(415) 750-0328

YES!
YOU CAN
STOP SMOKING Revised
"EVEN IF YOU DON'T WANT TO"

Copyright © 1996 David C. Jones

Edited by: Derick D. Schermerhorn
Cover Design by: Elaine Webber, Designs, Inc.

Published by Dolphin Publishing
Post Office Box 16656
West Palm Beach, Florida 33416
1-800-547-7867

ISBN 1-878400-02-9

Printed in the United States of America

TABLE OF CONTENTS

To my three beautiful daughters,
Deborah, Pam and Kathy.
I love you,
Dad

FROM THE AUTHOR

The original book, YES! YOU CAN STOP SMOKING, was an outstanding success. It did not break any sales records, nor was it on the talk shows. What it did do was to help people stop smoking. I received calls and spoke with people who bought my book and using the information, said that they were able to stop smoking and stay stopped. The book achieved its intended goal.

YES! YOU CAN STOP SMOKING Revised, is the same book, with a few changes. The ninety affirmations in the back of the book have been expanded. Some of the true–life stories have been replaced with new ones. The self–help section in the front has been updated and expanded.

I work with smokers on an inpatient basis. I see first hand what a powerful and devastating disease nicotine addiction is. Some smokers come to the program, have varied degrees of discomfort, stop smoking, and that's it. Then there are those who arrive with all the enthusiasm and motivation you could ask for. They honestly want to recover from their dependency. You know that these persons have tried to stop smoking many times in the past. You give them everything thing you have and more. You think that this time they are going to stop and stay stopped. They follow all the rules, do the assignments and participate in the groups. The next thing you know, the person says, "I just can't do this. I'm going home." The others in the program try to help their friend, but to no avail. The addiction is like a meat hook dragging its victim back into the frustration of smoking. The person is trapped within his or her own mind. Thoughts and emotions are being controlled by the addiction. The person appears unable to break the leash of dependence, even if it means death. The person has intense feelings of shame, guilt and frustration. The person leaves the program and goes back to smoking.

How do you fight such an affliction as this? I am not going to pretend that I know all of the answers. I do not. I am revising this book in an attempt to provide readers with the best information I can to help them stop smoking and recover from this awful illness.

Most of my knowledge about nicotine addiction comes from working with others. I have found that if you listen very closely, a person will tell you what his or her problem is and will also tell you what the solutions are. The trick is to listen, then to reflect that information back to the person so that he or she can apply that information to their recovery.

It is my sincere wish that you find the solutions that you are looking for. Thank you, and God bless.   *David Jones*

Chapter One

AM I ADDICTED TO NICOTINE?

If you smoke cigarettes or cigars, or use other tobacco products, and you want to stop, it is imperative that you understand what you are up against. There is a very good chance that you are addicted to the drug nicotine contained in these products. If this is true, then you are suffering from nicotine addiction, an extremely destructive illness that is progressive, incurable and terminal.

If you are unsure whether you are addicted or not, give yourself a simple test: Stop smoking. If you are unable to stay stopped and have to smoke to feel comfortable, then you probably are addicted.

There are varying degrees of this addiction. There are many people who smoke who are not addicted at all. These social smokers can put their cigarettes down and never smoke again. At the other end of the scale, there is the extreme dependent smoker who, no matter what he or she does, they cannot stop. Every year, thousands of smokers die as a result of their inability to stop smoking. For the "real addict," to stop smoking can be difficult at best. Some addicts become frustrated, angry, and desperate. Unfortunately, some become so discouraged that they give up and resign themselves to be smokers for the rest of their lives.

Addiction is a disease of denial. Denial is the mental defense mechanism that keeps the smoker from seeing the truth about his or her dependency. The person is not being dishonest. He or she actually does not see the truth. Smokers might verbalize that they are addicted but really think that they smoke because they enjoy smoking, or that smoking relaxes them. The smoker who is in denial of nicotine addiction will either continue to smoke or will seek out easy, painless methods to stop that do not address the real problem – the addiction. This is why so many smokers are unable to stop smoking or to stay stopped for any significant length of time.

Nicotine addicts spend millions of dollars on easy "quick-fix" gimmicks guaranteed to make them stop smoking, with only a few achieving long–term success. Smoking is often considered a moral issue and treated as a bad habit. Smokers are considered to have a lack of willpower.

> People have been told, "If you really want to quit, you will. If you don't stop, you really didn't want to stop in the first place." This statement sounds reasonable, but it is not accurate. You do not have to _want_ to stop smoking to become a non-smoker.

No addict wants to give up his or her drug of choice. That is what being addicted means. For the addict it is not a matter of just quitting smoking; it is a matter of recovering from the illness of nicotine dependency.

There are no easy remedies or "quick-fixes" for any addiction. The same is true of other addictions. Alcoholism, cocaine dependency and heroin addiction only respond to appropriate treatment. The reality is, of all these substances, nicotine is the most addictive drug there is.

With accurate information, you can break through your denial, dodge the quick-fix artist, make intelligent decisions about the direction of your recovery, and get down to the real issues at hand. You now have the opportunity to recover from your addiction and enjoy a life that is happy, joyous, and free.

Chapter Two

HOW DOES NICOTINE
AFFECT THE BODY?

There are many physical factors connected with a person's use of drugs. Drugs alter the normal functions of the human body. Nicotine is a powerful drug and has very significant effects. For example, nicotine constricts the blood vessels and stimulates the heart, resulting in increased blood pressure. When cigarette smoke enters the lungs, mucous is excreted to protect the tissues of the lungs from the toxicity of the smoke. This barrier impedes the exchange of oxygen into and the elimination of carbon dioxide out of the bloodstream. Carbon monoxide, a deadly poisonous gas produced by the burning of tobacco, is taken into the lungs and is absorbed into the bloodstream. This condition displaces the oxygen required for the proper functioning of the body's organs.

Smoking and other forms of nicotine use can be the direct cause of, or a major contributing factor to, many diseases. These include heart disease, stroke, embolism, high blood pressure, elevated cholesterol, osteoporosis, arteriosclerosis, Grave's disease, skin wrinkling, sexual dysfunction, lung cancer, brain cancer, cervical cancer, breast cancer, throat cancer, stomach cancer, tongue cancer, gum disease, emphysema, bronchitis, and diminished mental cognitive powers.

The number one physical consequence of smoking is heart disease. Nicotine promotes plaque buildup in the arteries and can clog them up, restricting the flow of oxygen-rich blood to the body's extremities and organs. This is particularly damaging to the muscles of the heart. If your heart does not get the oxygen-rich blood that it needs, it can be severely damaged and even stop. This, of course, can result in death.

> How often have you heard about "so-and-so" who is in the hospital having a triple bypass? Chances are, that person is a smoker.

Lung cancer is the other big killer of smokers. There is a denial about this disease that "it will not happen to me." The fact is, there are 172,000 new cases of lung cancer reported each year and 153,000 deaths from the disease. This is just one form of cancer a person can contract from the use of nicotine.

Some smokers think that they can beat the odds by using smokeless tobacco, such as snuff and chewing tobacco. This is a false illusion. Smokeless tobacco use can actually lead to a more severe nicotine dependency than smoking can. This form of nicotine use is markedly dangerous because the tobacco itself with all of its carcinogens comes into direct contact with the flesh in the mouth. A wad of tobacco will actually eat a hole or a pocket into the gum where the tobacco is placed. There is also a higher prevalence of oral cancer from tobacco chewing than there is of lung cancer from cigarette smoking.

Many young men use smokeless tobacco in place of smoking, thinking that it is safe and that it is the male thing to do. Unfortunately we are seeing young people in their teens and twenties with various types of mouth diseases, including mouth cancer. Have no illusions, *there is no safe way to use tobacco.*

The World Health Organization estimates that two million people in the world will die every year from diseases caused by smoking. More than 400,000 will be from the United States. Smoking kills more people each year than all other addictions combined, including cocaine addiction, heroin dependency and alcoholism. Tobacco-related diseases are the number one preventable cause of death in the United States today!

Smoking can cause penal artery disease in men that could lead to impotency. If a man smokes one pack of cigarettes per day for five years, his penal artery can be restricted by 50%. Smoking can also reduce stamina, further decreasing a person's sexual performance.

Smoking has a devastating impact on women. One function of the female hormone estrogen is to maintain bone mass. Smoking can cause reduced estrogen levels in women and can contribute to osteoporosis. Women who smoke could also start menopause two to five years earlier than women who do not smoke. Women smokers are less likely to become pregnant than nonsmokers.

It appears that women have a more difficult time stopping smoking than men. The reasons for this are not entirely clear. One theory is that women have more of a history of being discriminated against and of being abused. The drug nicotine helps suppress the emotions caused by this abuse, and when the person stops smoking, the feelings from these issues surface. The emotions of hurt, fear, anger, and depression are just too much. The person smokes in order to feel better. Men do the same thing, but they seem to be able to stop more easily than women.

Because nicotine constricts the blood vessels, and carbon monoxide displaces oxygen from the blood, the skin has a reduced supply of oxygen-rich blood. This condition can be a major factor in premature aging and skin wrinkling for both men and women. When you stop smoking your skin will recoup some of its smoothness and luster, and you will actually look younger.

Second-hand cigarette smoke also takes its toll. If you live with a smoker, you will probably suffer from some degree of respiratory discomfort. Your chances of contracting heart disease, lung cancer, emphysema and bronchitis are increased because of living in this form of air pollution.

Children are especially susceptible to second-hand smoke. As a fetus, the unborn child can be underweight, be born premature with underdeveloped lungs and heart, and have decreased learning abilities later in life. Children who live in a home where at least one person is a smoker are sick and absent from school more often than children from homes where they are not exposed to smoke. Children who become smokers almost always come from a home where at least one of the parents was a smoker.

It is estimated that 25% of deaths from fires, 30% to 40% of deaths from heart disease, 85% of deaths from lung cancer, and 85% of deaths from chronic obstructive lung disease are directly related to cigarette smoking.

The cost of healthcare to businesses resulting from smoking-related diseases exceeds $16 billion annually. Smoking also costs companies billions of dollars in lost production due to workers smoking on the job. Smokers have decreased earning abilities as they become disabled. A smoker's productive years and earning abilities can end way before his or her time due to contracting a smoking-related illness. The smoker is also more likely to die prematurely. For obvious reasons, smoking is a major problem to business. Companies prefer to hire employees that do not smoke.

The message I would like to convey is: Nicotine is a very powerful chemical. Its use, along with the tars, carcinogens, carbon monoxide and the other elements that go with nicotine, have profound, damaging effects. There is no way to use this addictive substance without eventually suffering consequences, some of which are irreversible.

When you stop smoking, your chances of contracting a chronic disease such as cancer, emphysema, bronchitis, arteriosclerosis and heart disease are substantially reduced. The symptoms of bronchitis clear up in a matter of days. You will feel better and have much more stamina.

The unseen consequences of smoking are the emotional feelings a smoker has toward himself or herself about being a smoker and not being able to stop. Everyone knows that smoking is physically harmful. It is against human nature for a person to do this harm to himself or herself and feel good about it.

A person who is unable to stop smoking can feel frustrated, helpless, and even hopeless. As a result, nicotine addiction can lead to feelings of low self-esteem.

Unfortunately, neither the physical nor the psychological consequences of smoking will deter a smoker from smoking until it is too late, and even then, the person might continue to smoke.

Chapter Three

WHAT IS NICOTINE ADDICTION?

> The human brain is a physical organ. The addiction to the drug nicotine is located in the brain. Therefore, nicotine addiction is a physical disorder.

This dependency can cause psychological problems or make existing mental problems worse, but the base of the disease itself is physical.

The tobacco in a cigarette is in a solid state. All the elements that make up the tobacco, including the drug nicotine, are harmless as long as they are in this state. When you light the end of your cigarette, you change the state of the tobacco from a solid to a gas. This unlocks all of the tobacco's elements. We call this gas cigarette smoke. The chemicals that made up the tobacco, including nicotine, are carried by this gas into the lungs. Because nicotine's chemical makeup is that of an alkaloid, it is compatible with the tissues of the lungs. The drug passes through the alveoli of the lungs and into the bloodstream where it goes to all parts of the body, including the brain. It takes about seven seconds for the drug to reach the brain.

Nicotine easily crosses the blood barrier of the brain and affects almost every neuron in it.

The brain is the control center of our entire being. It controls the heart, lungs, digestive system and virtually every function of the body. Within itself, the brain provides thinking, reasoning, memory and learning. The brain also controls emotions. Feelings might be sensed in the body, but they originate in the brain.

The brain provides these functions through a very complicated electrical and chemical process. These chemicals are called neurotransmitters. If you are in the middle of the road, and a truck is coming toward you, the sight of the truck enters your eyes. This stimulus travels to your brain and is perceived as a danger. The brain regulates its chemistry to cause you to feel fear. The fear motivates you to move out of the way of the truck. This process is part of the human survival system. When you are out of harm's way, your brain chemistry changes, and you feel relieved and safe. Without these defense mechanisms, human-kind would have died out a long time ago.

People have certain basic emotional needs. We all need to feel safe and secure. We need to have a general sense of well-being. If these basic needs are not met, we feel fear and anxiety. Some of the basic necessities that provide that secure feeling are air, food, water and shelter. There are other needs, of course, but these are the basics for human survival. As long as these needs are met, the brain releases the appropriate brain chemicals that provide the perception of security. If one of these needs is taken away, the brain perceives a threat, and you feel fear.

The drug nicotine stimulates the release of the same neurotransmitters that cause the sensation of feeling safe and secure. After smoking over a period of time, the brain that normally provides those feelings becomes chemically dependent on the drug nicotine to provide them. When you stop smoking, the brain is not going to just kick in and start working again. You are going to feel threatened and become hostile as a defense against the perceived threat. The brain is now in disorder. It regards nicotine as beneficial and the loss of the drug as threatening.

> The basic human necessities for survival are now considered by the brain to be air, water, food, shelter – and nicotine. This is nicotine addiction. The addict is driven by his or her basic survival instincts to smoke.

The most common denial of the smoker to his or her addiction is: "I like to smoke; it relaxes me. I smoke because I have so much stress in my life. I can stop anytime I want, I'm just not ready yet." Do not kid yourself.

> The only reason a nicotine addict smokes is because he or she is addicted to the drug nicotine.

Many people have stress in their lives, but they don't necessarily smoke. Nicotine is not a suppressant; it is a stimulant. The drug causes the release of those brain chemicals that give the illusion of relaxation and reduced stress. Nicotine increases the heart-rate and constricts the blood vessels, and carbon monoxide displaces the oxygen in the body.

> Cigarette smoking is a major source of stress, not the solution to stress.

It is important to say again that the real reason a nicotine addict smokes is because he or she is addicted to the drug nicotine.

> When the smoker can acknowledge and accept his or her addiction to the drug nicotine, practical solutions can be developed and the person can be successful at becoming a nonsmoker.

Chapter Four

WHAT MAKES NICOTINE ADDICTION A DISEASE?

Cigarette smoking is a symptom of the disease nicotine addiction. The word "addiction" is a medical diagnosis found in medical books. "The American Diagnostic and Statistical Manual of Mental Disorders IV," on page 243, specifically gives the diagnosis for compulsive smoking as "Nicotine Dependence." On page 244, The Manual describes nicotine-induced disorder as "Nicotine Withdrawal."

A disease has to have certain components that qualify it as an illness: *1. signs & symptoms, 2. progressive course, 3. diagnosis, 4. treatment (if available), 5. prognosis.* Sometimes a disease will have a family history. Nicotine addiction fits this profile of an illness precisely. There are five stages to the addiction, each gets progressively worse, and within those stages are signs and symptoms specifically related to the disease. The following pages describe these stages. Identify where you started, how far you have progressed, and where you are in your addiction today. This is a picture of your illness. It shows how far your addiction has progressed and where it is going to take you if it is not arrested. At first, the progression is slow. It may take years before any consequences become apparent. Once you start having chest congestion, poor circulation or a loss of stamina, the hand-writing is on the wall, and the consequences then progress at a much faster rate.

Along with the physical consequences of smoking, the addiction itself also progresses, making it harder and harder for you to stop smoking. The sooner you stop smoking, the easier stopping becomes. The more times that you go back to smoking after stopping, the more difficult it will be for you to stop again.

The Five Stages of Nicotine Addiction

INITIAL STAGE: Smokes first cigarette, probably in mid-teens; smokes because friends do; coughs, feels dizzy, eyes water, feels nauseous. Practices and builds up a tolerance for smoking. Feels mature, tough, cool, part of the crowd, independent and defiant. Experiments with various brands; smoking becomes part of identity; associates with others who smoke. At least one parent is a smoker. Smoking helps the young person deal with the stresses of school, teachers, parents and relationships; smoking makes life more tolerable. The young person becomes addicted to nicotine and may use other drugs.

ACCEPTANCE STAGE: Smoking is now accepted as part of daily life. The person smokes to talk on the telephone, drive, work, relax, have sex. Smokes before going to bed and upon waking. Smokes more when under emotional stress; smoking replaces regular coping skills; smokes a specific brand; keeps cigarettes in a designated place; becomes defensive if anyone says anything about smoking; most friends are smokers. At this point there are few consequences from smoking. The smoker is in denial of being addicted and thinks smoking-related illness happens only to others. The person rationalizes, "If I get that bad, I'll quit." The addiction is not addressed; continues to smoke.

CRUCIAL STAGE: Starts to lose the tolerance for smoking; has a loss of stamina; develops a cough and spits up phlegm. Develops early stages of smoking-related illnesses; contracts bronchitis and the early stages of emphysema; there may be some numbness and tingling in the fingers and toes; is at risk to heart attack or stroke. The smoker can no longer deny the consequences of smoking. Tries easy techniques to stop, but the addiction is not addressed; fails; has feelings of guilt, shame and hopelessness. Rationalizes, "I *must not be ready to stop smoking yet," and continues to smoke. As the addiction progresses, it becomes more difficult for the smoker to stop smoking.*

CRITICAL STAGE: Is in the middle to late stages of a smoking-related disease; has a significant loss of stamina and a loss of quality of life. The person might have heart disease, lung cancer, emphysema or chronic bronchitis. Life revolves around treating poor health; is spending hundreds of dollars on medication and medical bills. Has a degree of disability and may not be able to work. The person's life is in jeopardy. The person tries to stop smoking; the addiction is not addressed; continues to smoke. The person feels fear, shame, guilt, helpless despair, and hopelessness.

CHRONIC STAGE: Has the advanced stages of a smoking-related illness and is disabled; is on medication and probably oxygen; needs constant care for personal needs; has minimal quality of life. Feels fear, despair, helplessness, hopelessness, guilt, shame and humiliation. The last symptom of nicotine addiction is death.

Nicotine addiction meets the requirements for being a disease exactly. On the next page is a chart for The Five Stages of Nicotine Addiction.

THE FIVE STAGES OF NICOTINE ADDICTION

Progressive Course Downward

INITIAL STAGE: Smokes first cigarette; probably in mid-teens; smokes because friends do; coughs, feels dizzy, eyes water, feels nauseous. Practices and builds up a tolerance for smoke. Feels mature, tough, cool, part of the crowd, independent and defiant. Experiments with various brands; smoking becomes part of identity; associates with others who smoke. At least one parent is a smoker. Smoking helps the young person deal with the stresses of school, teachers, parents and relationships; smoking makes life more tolerable. The young person becomes addicted to nicotine and is susceptible to using other drugs.

ACCEPTANCE STAGE: Smoking is accepted as part of daily life. The person smokes to talk on the telephone, drive, work relax, have sex, before going to bed, upon waking up, etc. Smokes more under emotional stress; smoking replaces regular coping skills; smokes a specific brand; keeps cigarettes in a designated place; becomes defensive if anyone says anything about smoking; most friends are smokers. At this point there are few consequences from smoking. The smoker is in denial of being addicted and thinks smoking-related illness only happens to others. The person rationalizes "If I get that bad, I'll quit." The addiction is not addressed; continues to smoke.

CRUCIAL STAGE: Starts to lose the tolerance for smoke; has a loss of stamina; develops a cough and spits up phlegm. Develops early stages of smoking-related illness; contracts bronchitis and the early stages of emphysema; there may be some numbness and tingling in the fingers and toes; is at risk to heart attack or stroke. The smoker can no longer deny the consequences of smoking. Tries easy painless techniques to stop, but the addiction is not addressed; fails; has feelings of guilt, shame and hopelessness. Rationalizes *"I must not be ready yet,"* and continues to smoke. As the addiction progresses, it becomes more difficult for the smoker to stop smoking.

CRITICAL STAGE: Is in the middle to late stages of a smoking-related disease; has a significant loss of stamina and a loss of quality of life. The person might have heart disease, lung cancer, emphysema or chronic bronchitis. Life revolves around treating poor health; is spending hundreds of dollars on medication and medical bills. Has a degree of disability and may not be able to work. The person's life is in jeopardy. The person tries to stop smoking, but the addiction is not addressed; continues to smoke. The person feels fear, shame, guilt, helpless despair, and hopelessness.

CHRONIC STAGE: Has the advanced stages of a smoking-related illness and is disabled; is on medication and probably oxygen; needs constant care for personal needs; has minimal quality of life. Feels fear, despair, helplessness, hopelessness, guilt, shame and humiliation. The last symptom is death.

Mark on the chart where you see yourself. What does this tell about your future as a smoker?

Chapter Five

WHAT DOES IT MEAN TO BE "IN RECOVERY"

There are five stages to nicotine addiction. There are also five stages of recovery from the illness. Most new nonsmokers return to smoking because they are unaware of the pitfalls that lie ahead of them.

If you understand what is going to happen to you when you stop, if you know that what is happening is normal under the circumstances, and if you possess the skills to deal with those issues, you will not only stop smoking, you will stay stopped.

With this information you will be able to develop new healthy coping skills to deal with life on life's terms without the use of a drug.

Most smokers have smoked for years and expect to be able to stop with little or no pain. We all want the easy "quick-fix." Unfortunately, there are symptoms of recovery that are not always pleasant. Moreover, you cannot smoke for years and expect the addiction to go away overnight. Eighty to ninety percent of smokers who try to stop without accurate information relapse within one year.

Another concern in early recovery is not to exchange one addiction for another. For example, some of the obsessive compulsive behaviors ex-smokers tend to pick up are: *overeating, caffeine abuse, gambling, alcohol abuse, marijuana use, spending too much money, taking tranquilizers, oversleeping, obsessive working and excessive exercising.*

Cigarettes are an integral part of a smoker's life. When the addict stops smoking, it is like losing an old friend. When you take something this important out of your life, there is an emptiness or void that needs to be filled. For the addict, life revolves around smoking. Filling that hole left by this loss with new healthy coping skills is what is meant by being "In-Recovery."

On the following pages are "The Five Stages of Recovery from Nicotine Addiction." These stages represent the transition from smoker to nonsmoker. Having this knowledge about what the future holds will greatly reduce the difficulty of your recovery and will help you prevent relapse. Also, see the recovery chart at the end of this chapter. When people familiar with this information are asked what helped them the most with their recovery, most say this chart. Feel free to copy this chart and put it on your refrigerator door.

THE FIVE STAGES OF RECOVERY FROM NICOTINE ADDICTION

FEAR STAGE: *Anticipation of loss of cigarettes; feels threatened and insecure; stops smoking and has fear due to a chemical imbalance; fear of failure; fear of success; fear of withdrawal; fear of emotions; fear from anxiety or panic attacks; fear of going crazy or coming apart; fear from old unresolved issues surfacing.*

The fear stage keeps many smokers hooked until death. The closer the smoker gets to doing something about his or her smoking, the more intense the fear becomes. To help deal with this stage, first feel the emotions, then share them with a supportive friend. Accepting your feelings and being honest about them will greatly reduce their hold on you.

ADJUSTMENT STAGE: *Has stopped the intake of nicotine and starts withdrawal; feels angry, afraid, irritated, confused, tired; craves food and wants a cigarette; has to learn to talk, work, drive, eat, play, relax, communicate and deal with emotions without smoking; the lungs start to clean themselves out; spits up mucus; stamina improves; starts to feel better; will experience mood swings; withdrawal lasts about two weeks; after withdrawal, starts to feel better and could become* *complacent about recovery; feels like being on a pink cloud; could stop the recovery process; is in danger of relapse; thinks, "I can smoke just one"; experiences post-withdrawal symptoms at 30 days, 60 days and 90 days after cessation of nicotine; has symptoms of anger, confusion and craves a cigarette; post-withdrawal lasts from one to five days; becomes more assertive with others; self-esteem improves; starts to feel gratitude for recovery.*

This stage is more than just withdrawal – you will be emotionally vulnerable. After smoking for years, and now not having that shield, you will feel emotions like you never have before. There are some relapse causes in this stage that you need to be aware of: 1. Lack of skills to deal with withdrawal. 2. Complacency; being on a pink cloud and thinking you have it licked. Addicts are their own worst enemies. If things are going well, a false sense of security sets in, and the addict stops the recovery process and eventually smokes. If what you are doing works, keep doing it. 3. Inability to deal with feelings, especially fear and anger.

To help progress through this stage, seek out supportive friends. You may want to participate in a support group whose focus is on recovery from nicotine addiction. Get telephone numbers and call your supports regularly. You might also want to keep a daily journal. Write down some of the feelings you have during the day. What was the emotion, what was its source and how did you deal with it? Writing is excellent therapy that helps put those out-of-control feelings in their proper perspective.

ANGER STAGE: *Feels undefined anger; focuses on others' faults and becomes self-righteous; is irritable and hard to get along with; isolates and sleeps excessively; might become depressed; is unaware of underlying emotional issues; is in danger of relapse.*

In this stage, anger is the feeling on the surface. Old unresolved issues that had been suppressed for years by smoking are beginning to come to the surface. The anger is part of a defense mechanism that keeps the person from having to face the pain from those issues. The best way to deal with this stage is to talk with supportive friends. Also, write down the names of the people who are the source of your anger and how you feel toward those people today.

You might think that the emotional pain is not worth the effort and that you do not want to deal with these issues. In reality, the issues have always been there. You have been carrying them around for years, and they have been coming out in inappropriate ways and have had a negative effect on your life. They come out as relationship problems, work problems, low self-esteem, depression, and physical symptoms of headaches, backaches and stomach-aches.

You can go six months without a cigarette, then for no apparent reason start smoking. If you look close, you are probably experiencing the Anger Stage. If you have had some treatment in the past for those underlying emotional issues, the severity of this stage could be less severe.

GROWTH STAGE: *Feels the pain from the anger stage and chooses not to smoke; is willing to deal with past emotional issues; reaches out to others for help; has intense emotional ups and downs but is determined to take responsibility for self; accepts self as is; feels a sense of value; self-esteem soars; develops an intense gratitude for recovery; starts to feel mature; thinking becomes clear, focused and stable; sets new realistic goals; new doors of opportunity open.*

The Growth Stage and the Anger Stage go together. You're at a turning point in your recovery. You are feeling emotional pain, and you choose to not smoke. This is not an easy stage, but it is worth the effort. Those old issues have been haunting you far too long; now it's time to put them in their proper place. It is suggested that, if necessary, you seek help from a qualified therapist who specializes in treating your issues. You will find that your deepest pain can be your best source of emotional growth.

MAINTENANCE STAGE: *Smoking is no longer an issue; new healthy coping skills have replaced the need for nicotine; you participate in some form of support system; short and long-term goals are materializing; most friends are non-smokers; self-esteem soars and you have a sense of spirituality beyond description; you help others.*

This is the last stage, but your growth does not stop here. To be "in recovery" means that you continually improve the quality of your life. You will find that living nicotine-free is an adventure that is more exciting than any drug could ever be. Nicotine gives the user a false sense of security. Recovery allows you to be fully aware of yourself with all your trials, tribulations and joys. Without drugs, the path to personal growth is unlimited. You now have the opportunity to go as far as you choose.

The Five Stages of Recovery are meant to be a guide. If you cannot identify with everything, that's OK. The way to recovery is to acknowledge and accept the problem, then start living in the solutions. The solutions will involve change. If you go back to doing things as before without making some major changes for the better, you will smoke again. Remain open, teachable and willing to change, and you will be successful at becoming a nonsmoker. On the next pages are the approximate time frames for The Five Stages of Recovery.

TIME FRAMES FOR THE
FIVE STAGES OF RECOVERY

It is difficult to put time periods on the stages. Everyone is different, and what might take one person two weeks may take someone else a year or even longer. Also, you can be in more than one stage at a time. Listed below are some general time frames for the stages of recovery:

Fear Stage: *When you first decide to stop, you will feel anticipation and anxiety. After stopping the intake of nicotine, the fear usually disappears in about two weeks. By then you have gained some faith and self-confidence that you can do this. There may be times when you return to the fear stage, but if you make your recovery number one priority, the fear will pass.*

Adjustment Stage: *This stage takes the longest. You are changing a way of life, and that takes time. Not only will you be changing, but the people around you will have to adjust to the new you. It takes months, for many people more than a year, to adjust themselves to living without something to which they had become accustomed. Life itself is a matter of continual adjustment.*

Anger Stage: *The time frame for this stage depends on the degree of the severity of your past experiences. If you came from a reasonably stable background, it may take from one to eighteen months for this stage to appear. If you have had a* *very painful and traumatic history, this stage could begin anytime after day one. The average time that this stage hits is <u>about</u> seven months after the last use of nicotine.*

Growth Stage: *As mentioned earlier, the Anger Stage and the Growth Stage go together. You cannot stay in the Anger Stage very long without making a decision either to smoke or to get help. You will have to decide which you are going to do within two weeks after the Anger Stage has started. If you think you are going to need professional help, consider doing so before you stop smoking or soon after you stop. If you preempt the problem, these two stages will not be as severe.*

Maintenance Stage: *It takes about two years to <u>completely</u> make the transition from a smoker who is not smoking to a nonsmoker who feels like a nonsmoker.*

On the next page is the chart of The Five Stages Of Recovery From Nicotine Addiction.

MAINTENANCE STAGE: Smoking is no longer an issue; new healthy coping skills have replaced the need to smoke; new goals are met; there is a sense of wellness and a feeling of confidence within one's self. The addiction is not cured, but the person is in recovery and maintains that recovery on a daily basis. There is a feeling of gratitude and a desire to help others. As you give of yourself, you receive back ten-fold.

GROWTH STAGE: The person is feeling the pain from the Anger Stage and chooses not to smoke, but instead is willing to deal with the issues. The door for personal growth is open; proper help is obtained; there is a new awareness of self; develops feelings of serenity, peace, positive self-esteem and a sense of spirituality that is beyond definition.

ANGER STAGE: Old unresolved issues that have been suppressed for years are coming to the surface. These issues could go back to childhood. The person feels angry for no apparent reason; looks at others' faults; is defensive and hostile; isolates from others; has wide mood swings and has a sense of emotional confusion. The severity of this stage is in proportion to the severity of the past issues. Some of the feelings are: fear, anger, hurt, rejection, abandonment, betrayal, guilt, shame, remorse, resentment and low self-worth. The person could have a sense of being helpless, hopeless and can become depressed. At this point there is a tendency to isolate, sabotage the recovery process, dissolve positive relationships and smoke. To prevent relapse, it is important to reach out to friends and supports, and depending on the severity of the issues, it is suggested that professional help be sought.

ADJUSTMENT STAGE: Stops the intake of nicotine and begins withdrawal; experiences mood swings; has feelings of fear, anxiety, irritability, anger, depression and tiredness; feels vulnerable and cries for no reason; feels like a smoker who's not smoking; seeks support through friends and support groups; starts to feel better and has a sense of never wanting to smoke again; becomes complacent and stops the recovery process. The smoker is now ready to begin the adjustment period and is open to learning new coping skills to live life on life's terms and deal with daily issues without smoking. *Relapse causes: Denial of addiction, complacency and anger.* Experiences post withdrawal at 30 days, 60 days and 90 days; symptoms are: emotional confusion, anger and craving a cigarette; reaches out to supports; post withdrawal last less than a week; continues recovery.

FEAR STAGE: Makes plans to stop smoking; has feelings of anticipation, anxiety and insecurity; cannot imagine life without smoking. The fears come from: loss of nicotine; fear of failure; fear of success; fear of emotions from withdrawal, fear of emotions from old unresolved issues; fear of going crazy; fear of coming apart. Rationalizes why it's not the right time to stop smoking: "I'm not ready yet, I have to much stress, it's not in God's time, one addiction at a time, etc." The person has tried to stop many times in the past and failed. Looks for easy, painless techniques to stop. The person works through the fear, stops smoking and starts the recovery process. The healing can now begin.

THE FIVE STAGES OF RECOVERY FROM NICOTINE ADDICTION

Recovery Gets Progresively Better

The Five Stages tell you where you are in your recovery and where you are going.

Chapter Six

IS ONE PERSON MORE ADDICTED THAN ANOTHER?

Yes, one person can be more addicted to nicotine than another. There are some people who smoke who are not addicted at all. They can stop smoking anytime they want. These "social smokers" have little understanding of the true addict. The addict has even less understanding of the social smoker.

The earlier you address the addiction, the easier it is to deal with. If you continue to smoke, your brain can become so dependent on the drug that when you do try to stop, it will be as if your whole life is coming apart. The severity can be in direct relationship to how much and for how long a person has smoked.

There are other factors that can influence the severity of a person's dependency. Nicotine addicts have varying degrees of discomfort from nicotine withdrawal. Some people put their cigarettes down, experience mild discomfort, and that's the end of it. There are others who stop smoking and literally go crazy. Everyone else is somewhere in between the two extremes. Why does one person have such a different reaction to the cessation of smoking than another? Part of the answer is that one person's body may metabolize substances differently than another person's. Therefore, different people may have different body responses when giving up the drug.

Another explanation is that people are an accumulation of their past and present experiences. Nicotine can play a direct role in controlling how a person perceives those experiences. When a person stops smoking, past realities might not be recognized on a cognitive level, but will be felt emotionally. If the past issues were traumatic, then the nicotine-suppressed feelings could be extreme.

Cigarette smokers have different sets of specific commonalties that can be used to predict the variations and the severity of their withdrawal symptoms. Using these four profiles, you can pre-determine which classification you might come under, what the relapse reasons are, and what type of treatment will best help you recover from your addiction and prevent relapse. Review the profiles on the next page and identify the one that most closely pertains to you. (Note: you can be between two classifications.)

Minimal Dependency, Dependent, Severe Dependency, and Extreme Dependency

MINIMAL DEPENDENCY: *1. Has little or no history of family dysfunction. 2. Had a reasonably stable childhood. 3. Is goal-orientated and is successful at most endeavors. 4. Made good grades in school and has some degree of higher education. 5. Has adequate communication skills. 6. Interacts on a regular basis with close friends who have a similar background. 7. Is mentally stable, self-confident, secure, and has a healthy self-esteem.*

This person has smoked moderately for many years and has probably attempted to stop smoking more than once. He or she will continue to try to stop and might use some form of cessation program. The minimal dependent person can be one of those who can lay their cigarettes down, walk away and just not smoke anymore. There will be moderate withdrawal symptoms: irritability, confusion, loss of memory, tiredness, weight gain and the craving for a cigarette. The person will seek support from friends, get involved in some activity to keep the mind off smoking, and choose not to smoke. This person may from time to time smoke one or two cigarettes and stop. This smoker is more an abuser than an addict. He or she will feel good about being a nonsmoker, and staying away from cigarettes is not a major problem.

DEPENDENT: *1. At least one of the person's parents was a smoker. 2. There is some history of dysfunction in the family (possibly addiction). 3. There may have been some past childhood abuse or neglect. 4. Had at least one positive role model. 5. Most of the person's friends are smokers. 6. The person is compulsive and may have another addiction. 7. Has some difficulty with confidence and self-esteem. 8. Is moderately successful in most endeavors. 9. Smoking is primarily used to deal with stress. 10. Has fair communication skills. 11. Likes physical activity. 12. Is easy to like.*

Smoking is normal for this person. The nicotine may be masking some past emotional issues, but most of the time smoking is used to suppress the daily stresses of living. This person will have a difficult time stopping because smoking is seen as beneficial and enjoyable – so why stop?

Relapse Causes: Denial of smoking as a drug addiction; complacency; lack of motivation; lack of coping skills for dealing with stress; old unresolved issues could surface after a short period of abstinence; could pick up a cigarette without being aware of the feelings causing the relapse.

Recovery Recommendations: Learn about smoking as a drug addiction; learn about the consequences of smoking; learn new healthy stress management skills; take a course on assertive communications; exercise regularly; develop a support system that includes positive friends and a support group whose focus is on the recovery from nicotine addiction. This person would do well in a cessation program and would benefit from counseling for unresolved issues. If there is a relapse, don't throw the whole program away; put the cigarettes down, and call your supports.

SEVERE DEPENDENCY: *1. Comes from a dysfunctional family of either mental illness, alcoholism or drug addiction. 2. At least one parent smokes. 3. Experienced verbal abuse and possibly physical abuse as a child. 4. Seldom feels like part of a group. Feels different from others. 5. Could have another addiction and is probably co-dependent. 6. Is compulsive. 7. Has low self-esteem and lacks self-confidence. 8. Maintains a subtle defensive posture. 9. Has difficulty in relationships. 10. Is intelligent, creative and hard-working yet feels inadequate. 11. Has difficulty maintaining concentration and has a scattered thought process. 12. Is a people-pleaser and caretaker. 13. Cannot imagine life without smoking. 14. Has difficulty identifying and expressing feelings. 15. Has suppressed feelings of anger, resentment, guilt, shame, etc. 16. Could suffer from depression.*

The severe dependent has probably smoked since mid-teens or earlier. This person smokes because he or she is addicted to nicotine, but also uses the drug to suppress the pain of underlying emotional issues. This individual could also have another chemical addiction, eating disorder, codependency and/or depressive disorder. The smoker may be using nicotine as medication for any one of these problems.

This person will try many times to stop smoking, without success. The withdrawal could be severe. The symptoms might be: undefined fear, anger, depression, anxiety, panic, confusion, memory loss, tiredness, skin crawling, sleep disturbances, craving food, and craving a cigarette. The Severe Dependent has little tolerance for emotional pain and will look for easy quick fixes to stop smoking. When the person attempts to stop and fails, the person will compare himself or herself to those who can quit easily and without difficulty. This comparison reinforces the existing sense of inadequacy and validates the feelings of inferiority. Without the proper treatment and support, this person has a marginal chance of recovery. (Note: The person may stop smoking but without the proper help could also switch to another obsessive compulsive behavior.)

Relapse Causes: Lacks knowledge of smoking as a drug addiction; lacks skills for dealing with withdrawal; lacks coping skills for daily stresses; has difficulty dealing with current and old emotional issues (especially hurt, fear and anger); suffers from another disorder and needs nicotine to medicate the symptoms; isolates himself or herself from others and needs a cigarette for comfort; denial of recovery needs; lack of knowledgeable professional help; does not follow through with recovery plans.

Recovery Recommendations: The person should learn as much as possible about his or her dependency; participate in a support group for nicotine addiction; seek supportive friends and call them on a regular basis; maintain a regular but moderate exercise program; go on a proper diet; get enough sleep; work a reasonable number of hours and take time to have fun. The most important recommendation is to seek professional help for any other underlying disorder. Seek help from a therapist who understands the issues and is aware that smoking is a drug addiction and that addiction is an illness. Consider having a psychiatric evaluation.

On occasion, the Severe Dependent could experience anxiety or panic attacks, as well as periods of depression. Sometimes it can be beneficial to take a nonaddictive medication for those symptoms. This can give the person a window of time so that the addiction can be addressed while the person receives therapy for the second disorder. If you are reluctant to take medication, remember that you've been using your nicotine as a medication all these years, so you might as well use one that is appropriate. Be open to taking medication on your doctor's advice.

EXTREME DEPENDENCY: *1. Has at least one parent or guardian who was alcoholic, drug addicted or mentally ill. 2. As a child, he or she was verbally and possibly physically abused. This person might also have been a victim of sexual abuse. 3. There was probably no one to turn to for help as a child. 4. Feels alone, betrayed, abandoned, angry, enraged, afraid, confused, guilty, and ashamed. 5. Also feels inadequate, unworthy, has low self-esteem and lacks self-confidence. 6. Has thought of and may have attempted suicide. 7. Has another addiction, is co-dependent, and probably suffers from depression. 8. Has difficulty with self-identity, achieving goals and developing own opinions. 9. Has constant problems in relationships. 10. Does not trust others. 11. Has difficulty identifying and expressing feelings. 12. Maintains a subtle but constant defensive posture. 13. Has difficulty getting along with others at work. 14. Suffers from physical problems such as backaches, headaches, stomachaches and in general feels tired and run down. 15. Sleeps excessively. 16. Isolates from others. 17. Tends to overeat. 18. May be taking addictive medication.*

The person who suffers from Extreme Nicotine Dependency uses the drug primarily to medicate one or more emotional disorders. When the intake of nicotine is stopped, the underlying illness will surface within a matter of days and the person could have a psychotic episode. This episode could manifest itself as anxiety or panic attacks. The person might experience undefined fear, anxiety, paranoia, anger, rage, confusion, loss of memory and could become dysfunctional. The person could develop a rash. He or she will sleep excessively in order to numb feelings. The person might even consider suicide.

Relapse causes: The underlying disorder surfaces, the person relives old painful experiences and needs nicotine to medicate the emotional pain; isolates; lacks skills for dealing with withdrawal; lacks basic stress management skills; angers easily, resists reaching out for help; does not feel worthy of recovery; feels like a failure and gives up; lacks knowledgeable, professional help; denies smoking as a drug addiction; feels complacent; does not follow through with recovery plans.

Recovery Recommendations: Learn as much as possible about nicotine addiction and underlying disorders; seek treatment from a qualified therapist for underlying issues; avoid those who recommend that you smoke; ask for a psychological evaluation; ask your therapist to help you learn new healthy coping skills for dealing with fear and anger; discuss with your doctor possible options for taking nonaddicting antidepressant medication; if medication is prescribed, take it; avoid quick fixes; participate in a nicotine addiction recovery program in an inpatient or outpatient setting; participate in a support group where the focus is on recovery from nicotine addiction; develop a network of supportive friends and call them regularly. It is essential that the Extreme Dependent person maintain a moderate exercise program on a regular basis; eat properly; sleep an adequate number of hours, but do not sleep excessively; work a reasonable number of hours; take time to have fun.

Special Danger Areas

> Beware of depression; do not isolate yourself from others. Watch out for complacency; don't be your own worst enemy. Follow through with your recovery plans and your therapist's suggestions.

Wide mood swings are common and will seem as if they will last forever. They won't. No matter what your emotions are, they will pass. Feel the feelings and talk about them with supportive friends.

If you relapse, keep in mind that addiction is not a moral issue. You're not a bad person because you picked up a cigarette. Put it down and reach out for help. Any success that you have achieved you do not lose. Turn a relapse into a positive. What did you learn and how can you use that information for your recovery? If you are on medication do not stop taking it until your therapist and doctor tell you to. Never give up!

SUMMARY

In the past, all smokers were treated the same. The Extreme Dependent person was treated with the same techniques as the Minimal Dependent person. When the Extreme Dependent person was not successful at recovery, he or she was accused of not wanting to stop smoking, or of being lazy and dishonest. This approach indicates a lack of knowledge about nicotine addiction and is counter-productive to recovery. The addict already feels bad; inconsiderate treatment by uninformed people only reinforces existing inner feelings of inade-quacy.

These four classifications are totally different from each other and require different approaches.

One thing holds true for all addicts: scolding, nagging, guilt trips and talking down to the person does harm.

To help a smoker stop, you must look beyond the cigarette to the person on the other side. The cigarette is like the tip of the iceberg – it's but a symptom of the underlying issues.

If you treat only the cigarette and ignore the addiction and other issues, the smoker will have no choice but to return to using nicotine. It's just a matter of time.

Use these profiles like a crystal ball. They tell you what is coming and what can be done to reduce the impact of relapse. A relapse can be preempted and prevented if you receive treatment before the symptoms arise. If you need therapy for traumatic past issues, get that treatment either before you stop smoking or at the time of cessation.

It is not unusual for people to say, "I saw a therapist about those issues a long time ago. I've dealt with them." If you were smoking at the time of that treatment, there will still be some residual baggage left over that was suppressed by the use of nicotine. You will need additional care at some point. Those past problems will resurface. However, because of your past therapy, those issues will probably not be as severe as they would have been if you had not had previous help.

Chapter Seven

THE BENEFITS OF BECOMING A NONSMOKER

If a person stops smoking and there are no benefits, why stop? Fortunately there *are* benefits for becoming a nonsmoker. The first reward is the freedom to choose to not smoke. The second is an increase in positive self-esteem.

The physical benefits are almost immediate. The congestion in your lungs clears up rapidly and you can breath better. The blood vessels open up, the heart slows down and your blood pressure lowers. Here is a list of some of the benefits of becoming a nonsmoker:

Increased stamina	Clearer complexion
Positive personal growth	Improved dental health
Improved breathing	Less stress
Lower pulse	Better immune system
Lower cholesterol	Less sickness
Improved sense of smell	Awareness of feelings
Improved circulation	Good health
Improved eyesight	Quality way of life
Improved sense of taste	Younger appearance
Lower blood pressure	Money savings
Better skin sensitivity	Positive self-esteem
Improved sex life	Longer life

As a nonsmoker you will also be less susceptible to other diseases, such as lung cancer, heart disease, emphysema and bronchitis. The physical benefits of becoming a nonsmoker are obvious.

Everyone knows smoking is bad for you – it says so right on the pack. What most smokers do not know is how much smoking changes their sense of reality.

> Nicotine is a stimulant in every way except one: it has the effect of suppressing emotional awareness.

Daily emotional issues are hidden under a cloud of smoke and become inner stress. Old unresolved issues, some going back to childhood and thought to have been dealt with, continually surface and sabotage the quality of daily living.

> The constant concealing of your thoughts and emotions with a drug such as nicotine can be a source of depression and low self-esteem.

Becoming a nonsmoker dissolves the barriers of addiction and gives you the opportunity to address daily issues. In addition, that old emotional baggage can now be put to rest once and for all.

When the door of nicotine addiction is closed, new doors of personal awareness and emotional growth open. This benefit alone is well worth the effort of becoming a nonsmoker.

Chapter Eight

HOW TO DEAL WITH FEELINGS

Feelings, moods and emotions are all the same thing. To feel is to have an internal response to an event with regard to the perceptions of what that event means to the individual. Perceptions come from past experiences. The response to any current event is based on those experiences and by how a person feels toward himself or herself at present. Feelings are felt in the body, but they originate in the brain where all of those old perceptions are stored.

If you have a poor self-image and lack self-confidence, then you will probably experience fear more often and to a greater degree than a person who has a positive self-image and healthy self-esteem.

The differences in the two people are influenced by each individual's past experiences.

A child who had been continually punished for getting angry could grow up suppressing his or her anger until it builds up to such a degree that the person explodes in a fit of rage. This reaction is usually out of proportion to the issue and is often directed toward an innocent person. One might also express anger in indirect, subtle ways, such as by using sarcasm, kidding, being constantly late, making mistakes, gossiping, being manipulative, and blaming others for life's problems. The person is usually unaware of this hidden anger and of the fact that this passive-aggressive behavior is at the root of his or her problems with other people.

We learn to express our feelings starting in childhood. If you had been continually told, "You shouldn't feel that way," or, "Don't you dare get angry with me, young man," you might grow up not knowing how you should feel, and you might think that what you do feel is not legitimate.

If you were raised in a home where your parents called you stupid and perhaps compared you with your brother or sister, you could grow up thinking that you are not quite as good as others. This type of treatment could also cause you to be self-conscious. Any criticism from others will only reinforce how you have already been taught to feel about yourself – "stupid."

If a person grows up in a home where one or both parents are abusive, the child has to develop survival mechanisms to weather the ordeal. Normal emotional development can not take place. Instead, the child has to find ways to suppress the hurt, fear and anger that result from such treatment. Those defenses might be necessary for survival at the time, but they can leave the person an emotionally confused cripple for many years later. Some people actually say that their feelings are frozen in time.

> The long-term effect on a person from a dysfunctional environment is that the person can grow up into adulthood with perceptions and communication skills of a child.

The sad fact is that many people live their entire lives as adult-children. If these people do not receive some form of help, they pass their negative behaviors on to their children.

> Smoking cigarettes is another one of those unhealthy defense mechanisms that keeps a person emotionally stuck.

Nicotine masks fear and anger and gives the user a chemically-induced sense of well-being. It is not unusual for a smoker to stop smoking, and even though that person is physically an adult, he or she feels emotionally like a child. Regardless of your past history, if you have been smoking for a long period of time you will probably have difficulty getting in touch with and expressing your feelings.

Here is an exercise that will help you learn to identify and express your feelings appropriately. Take a piece of paper and make four columns. In the first column make the heading FEELINGS; in the second, write SOURCE; the third, REACTION; and in the last, write POSITIVE RESPONSE OPTIONS. Every day, fill out the chart with some of the feelings that you experienced during the day. Write down who or what the source of each feeling was, then how you reacted. In the last column, write out how you could have handled the problem differently. Don't worry if you do it wrong. The object is to learn from your mistakes. Your latent problem-solving skills will tell you what you could have done. If you have difficulty thinking of options, ask a friend to help you. When you write your options down, you will remember them and use them the next time you run into a similar situation.

Suppose you do not know how you feel. That's not unusual for addicts in early recovery. Try starting your list with the REACTION column first. Be objective. What feeling do you think a person would be trying to express who used that particular behavior? Example: If you yell at someone, it's obvious the feeling is anger. Now write down in the SOURCE column what the person did. Ask yourself, "How did that person's behavior affect me?" If what the person did was threatening, was fear the feeling behind the anger? Try to write as much as you can. Your own common sense will take care of the rest. (Use the feelings list on page 50 to help you.)

Here are a few more suggestions that will help you deal with your emotions: First, identify your feelings the best you can, then accept them; take "personal ownership." Remember that your feelings come from your perceptions. Now, practice feeling your feelings. The tendency will be to deny or suppress the emotions. That's what your smoking helped you do. To practice this skill, sit down, uncross your arms and legs, and get in touch with your breathing. You might unconsciously stop breathing, or swallow; this suppresses the emotions. Breathe normally and don't swallow. Allow the emotion to come up, and feel the feeling. At first the feeling will come over you like a wave, then it will subside. This will seem strange at first, but you will come to enjoy the experience of feeling your emotions. As you practice this skill, you will become in charge of your feelings instead of being out of touch and emotionally out of control.

Once you have experienced your feelings, it is time to learn how to express them. Take a course or buy a book on assertive communications.

The key things to remember are: Identify the feelings, feel the emotions, then own them.

To express yourself, start your sentences with "I" statements. "I feel angry," not, "You make me feel angry." The second example is judgmental and blaming. This indicates that you think the other person is responsible for your emotional well-being. That's not honest. In the first example, you are taking ownership for the emotion by using an "I" statement to express yourself. In other words, you are taking responsibility for your feelings. Of all the benefits of becoming a nonsmoker, learning to express yourself appropriately is one of the most gratifying and will lead to healthy self-esteem.

Below is a list of emotions to help you identify how you feel. There is also space for you to make notes or write down other emotions you might experience during your early recovery.

Love	Anger	Emptiness
Hate	Frustration	Hurt
Joy	Sadness	Loneliness
Envy	Lust	Confidence
Shame	Compassion	Loss
Excitement	Helplessness	Betrayal
Serenity	Empathy	Silliness
Sorrow	Remorse	Relief
Grief	Guilt	Rejection
Resentment	Hopelessness	Anxiety
Self-pity	Abandonment	Panic
Happiness	Rage	Gratefulness
Peace	Jealousy	Depression

What other feelings can you add to the list?

_____

_____

_____

_____

_____

_____

_____

Chapter Nine

WHAT IS NICOTINE WITHDRAWAL?

Nicotine withdrawal is the physical and mental discomfort experienced when a person addicted to nicotine stops the intake of the drug. After using nicotine over a period of time, it is normal for a person to feel the way he or she does when using it.

When the person stops taking the drug, the person will feel abnormal until the body can detoxify the nicotine out of the system and adjust itself to feeling normal without the drug.

Nicotine is a stimulant that increases the heart rate and speeds up the digestive system. It also causes the release of certain hormones that bring the body to a constant state of readiness. The carbon monoxide from the burning of the tobacco in a cigarette displaces the oxygen in the blood, while the nicotine constricts the blood vessels. This causes an increase in blood pressure and an oxygen deficiency to all parts of the body, including the heart, lungs and other organs. The nerve endings of the skin are deprived of oxygen, suppressing the skin's sensitivity. Cigarette smoke causes the lungs and airways to secrete mucus to protect the tissues from the toxicity of the smoke, and contributes to obstructive pulmonary disorder.

When smoking is stopped, the heart and lungs slow down, the blood vessels open, and the person feels tired and lethargic. The digestive system is no longer stimulated by the nicotine, so it slows down and the person may become constipated. Oxygen-rich blood now flows to the nerve endings, and the skin feels as if it is crawling. The lungs and airways no longer need all that mucus for protection, so the person starts to spit up phlegm as the lungs clean themselves out. That "smoker's cough" will probably get worse before it gets better. The throat could also become sore as its raw tissue becomes exposed.

This physical withdrawal from nicotine lasts for about two weeks. The worst period is the first three days.

Listed below are some of the most common symptoms of physical withdrawal. These symptoms are normal when you stop smoking.

Feeling tired	Craving food
Lethargy	Diarrhea
Skin crawling	Nausea
Aching joints	Sweats
Dizziness	Spitting up phlegm
Constipation	Headaches
Queasiness	Skin rash

There are also episodes of post-withdrawal. During these post-withdrawal episodes the new nonsmoker will feel undefined anger and confusion, and will crave a cigarette.

Many recovering addicts relapse during the post-withdrawal period because they are unaware of what is happening to them.

The person feels as if the discomfort will last forever and thinks, "If this is what not smoking is all about, I want no part of it." Post-withdrawal episodes normally occur at 30, 60 and 90 days after stopping the intake of nicotine. These episodes last from one to three days. Just knowing that these symptoms are normal and that they will pass greatly reduces their severity.

There is also a mental withdrawal from nicotine. For more detailed information about the effects of nicotine on the mind, see the chapter, "What is Nicotine Addiction?" on page 12. The brain becomes chemically dependent on the drug nicotine to supply the sensation of feeling safe and secure. Nicotine masks fear and anger. When a smoker stops smoking, these two feelings are dominant. These feelings can be so intense the person could relapse within a short period of time.

Since the brain is a physical organ, the effects of nicotine on it are physical. The drug alters the brain's chemistry that controls how a person feels.

Occasionally when a person stops the intake of nicotine, he or she will experience extreme emotional instability. This condition could take the form of anxiety or panic attacks, paranoia, confused thinking, depression and, for some, suicidal thoughts. Obviously, there is something more than nicotine withdrawal happening when a person is having these types of symptoms. This person could have a second disorder masked by the nicotine. (See the chapter, "Is One Person More Addicted Than Another?" on page 31.) An underlying depressive disorder may surface when the person stops smoking. If this happens, it is a good idea for the person to seek professional help. If antidepressant medication is prescribed, follow your doctor's advice.

It is important to keep in mind that these problems are not moral issues, nor are they about being strong, weak, worthy or unworthy.

At the time, you might feel that you're the worst person on earth. You're not. Those negative feelings are symptoms of the problem.

A depressive disorder is an illness, just like any other illness. You deserve to receive proper help and to live a happy life. Get the help you need.

When you are withdrawing from nicotine, you are going to be uncomfortable. It will seem as though your distress will last forever. You'll go through all kinds of ups and downs, and you'll wonder if becoming a nonsmoker is worth it. Your brain will come up with rationalizations as to why you should go back to smoking. Don't believe them. The addiction is lying to you.

Below is a list of mental symptoms you might experience when you stop smoking. Don't let these symptoms scare you. You will not have all of them, and the ones you do have will pass. You will be OK! You can greatly reduce the severity of your withdrawal by using the suggestions in Chapter Fifteen, "How to Stop Smoking" on page 74.

Undefined fear	Confusion
Anxiety	Frustration
Anger	Depression
Panic	Crying
Irritability	Craving food
Impatience	Sleep disturbance
Memory loss	Craving a cigarette

Write down any other symptoms that you have.

_____

_____

_____

_____

_____

_____

_____

_____

_____

Chapter Ten

WILL I GAIN WEIGHT WHEN I STOP SMOKING?

When you stop smoking, you will probably gain weight. The reason you gain weight is because nicotine is a stimulant that speeds up the body's functions, causing the body to burn more calories. When you stop smoking, your body slows down and requires fewer calories. If you eat the same amount of food after you stop smoking as you did before you stopped, you will gain weight.

Statistics tell us the average weight gain for a person who stops smoking is five pounds. If that figure pertains to you, great! However, if you happen to be one of those who tend to put on twenty pounds or more, statistics are of little comfort.

You might also gain weight because of the effect nicotine has on various organs of the body, such as pancreas. Nicotine suppresses the output of insulin by the pancreas. When a person stops smoking, there is a rebound effect, and an excess of insulin floods the blood-stream. Insulin is used by the body to process sugar in the blood. If there is an excess amount of insulin, you will have a sugar deficiency. Your body will crave those foods that can supply it with the sugar it needs to use up the additional insulin.

Another reason you might gain weight is that processed sugar releases some of the same brain chemicals as nicotine that give the user a similar sense of well-being. The tendency will be to eat sweets. The sugar will cause an emotional high, and when you crash off that high, you will crave a cigarette to bring you back up. You not only gain weight, but you're back smoking again. If all of this seems unfair, it is.

For the nicotine addict, fear of gaining weight can reinforce and justify a decision to return to smoking. Do not allow that fear to sabotage your goal. There are realistic solutions.

When you crave sweets, eat fruit. The fructose in fruit is sugar but is not as concentrated as processed sugar. In its natural state, fructose is in fiber form, so most of it goes right through you.

As for the excess insulin, eat complex carbohydrates. Foods such as pasta, bread, grains and vegetables enter the digestive system and are converted into glucose, another form of sugar needed for energy and the proper functioning of the body. The difference is, glucose is metered into the bloodstream as needed. What is not used changes into a chemical called glycogen that is stored in the body's organs and tissues for later use. When you need energy, the glycogen converts back into glucose. This is the same diet used by today's athletes.

You might have the desire to chew on something. Try sugarless gum, carrot sticks or cinnamon sticks. Also, drink a lot of ice water. Water seems to reduce the cravings for cigarettes, and it aids in weight reduction. Avoid foods that contain large amounts of fat, as that is what the weight comes from.

> Exercise is essential for not gaining weight when you stop smoking.

One of the benefits of not smoking is that you have more stamina. Use this new energy to your advantage. If you have not exercised on a regular basis, take it easy. Start out slowly or you risk injury. See your physician before starting any new exercise program.

An excellent form of exercise is walking. If you walk at a normal pace for twenty minutes, you will have walked about one mile. If you can work yourself up to thirty minutes to an hour, three or four times per week, you will lose weight. At first you will not see any results, but hang in there. Your weight will seem to reposition itself, then the pounds will slowly come off and stay off. Develop a program that also includes flexibility and strength training. Muscles burn calories; fat does not. You can tone your muscles without looking muscular.

Muscle toning speeds up your metabolism, and you will burn more calories, even when you're sitting.

> Whatever you do, don't go on a quick-fix diet. Those gimmicks will get you the same results as the quick fixes for smoking – nowhere.

Another reason you might gain a few pounds is that nicotine can artificially keep your weight below what it is supposed to be. When you stop smoking, your body will seek its normal set point.

> At first your body will rebound, and you will gain more weight than you want. If you use common sense, your weight will drop back to where it should be.

There is a more serious reason a person might put on weight. Nicotine can partially mask an eating disorder. Smoking will not keep the weight off forever. Eventually, you will be an overweight smoker. Using one addiction to treat another only keeps you on that merry-go-round of frustration and low self-esteem. An eating disorder is a separate issue from nicotine addiction. If you suffer from a food addiction, continue your recovery for nicotine dependency, and get the separate help you need for the eating disorder.

> Most people who stop smoking gain some weight, but they take it off as their bodies adjust to being nicotine-free and as they make the necessary life changes to maintain their recovery.

Chapter Eleven

HOW CAN MY RECOVERY BE SABOTAGED?

Before and after you stop smoking, you will run into a maze of obstacles that are going to threaten your recovery from nicotine addiction. If you are going to be successful at becoming a nonsmoker, you must be aware of these dangers, be willing to make your recovery your number one priority, and do what is necessary to stay out of harm's way.

The first threat is yourself. The brain is addicted to nicotine. Therefore, it sees smoking as beneficial and the loss of cigarettes as threatening. Your brain is thinking in reverse.

If your addiction is threatened, you will automatically defend yourself. Most of these defenses come as rationalizations motivated by the fear of losing the drug. On the next page are some common rationalizations that you might be able to identify with.

"The problem is, I enjoy smoking."

*"I can stop anytime I want.
I'm just not ready yet."*

"The only way to stop is on your own. You have to be strong and do this yourself. It's mind over matter."

"I can't stop right now. I have too much stress in my life. Anyway, smoking relaxes me."

"I can't give up everything. I'm going to die someday anyway, so what's the difference?"

"I'm afraid that if I stop, I'll come apart."

"If I stop smoking, I'll gain weight."

"Cancer doesn't run in my family. My father smoked all his life and never got lung cancer."

"They haven't proved that smoking is harmful."

"If the doctor tells me that I have three spots on my lungs, then I'll quit."

*"It's just not the right time," or,
"One addiction at a time."*

These defenses are automatic and normal for the addict whose drug use is threatened. They can also keep you stuck in the throes of your addiction. This is why it is so important to have supports.

> You will have to trust other people's thinking for a while until you can get some recovery time under your belt and start thinking clearly for yourself. Your supports will keep you centered and in touch with reality.

Another serious threat to your recovery will be from your spouse or "significant other." On the surface, that person will be supportive at first, but as you progress in your recovery, you are going to change. You will be irritable while going through withdrawal, but you will also be changing as a person. You will no longer be altering your emotions with a cigarette.

> You will be more honest about how you feel. Your partner will feel threatened by the new you.

Some things you might hear are: "You're a bitch – I liked you better when you were smoking! Now that you've stopped, can't you have just one or two, just to get you through the day?" Your partner does want you to stop smoking, but at the same time, the dynamics of living with an addict for a long period of time can sometimes dictate subtle negative behaviors that can sabotage recovery. This is not a good, bad, or moral issue. It is a symptom of addiction.

Sometimes, others with good intentions will try to manipulate your environment so that you won't get upset and smoke. Such people have a need to help or "fix" others. This type of behavior is demeaning and irritating. Ask them to stop.

If your significant other is also a smoker, you need to know that your chances of maintaining your recovery are significantly reduced. When you stop smoking, that person's addiction will be threatened by your success. His or her defense mechanisms will surface to resist the threat.

The tendency will be for you to try to explain and make the other person understand what you are doing and that smoking is a drug addiction. You are setting yourself up for rejection and failure. The other person is not in the same "space" you are in. He or she will start arguments, yell, even throw things, or give you the silent treatment. You will be called "self-righteous." The smoker will also pick apart your program and any information you offer.

Chances are, you will become hurt, discouraged, and angry. At this point you might smoke to cover up your hurt feelings.

Be smart – do not feed into any negativity. Keep the focus on your recovery, and accept others as they are. Remember, their behavior is motivated by their fear of your success. You're going to have to let go and practice patience, understanding and tolerance.

> For you to stay successful at being a nonsmoker while living with a smoker, you must seek support outside of your usual environment.

When the pressure at home gets to be too much, "detach" – walk around the block or call a supportive friend. You will be surprised how things will change when you no longer react to some one else's behavior by smoking.

The next threat to your recovery can come from smokers at work. You will find that there are some very insecure people who will feel threatened by what you are doing. They might taunt you by offering you a cigarette, talk down to you – even blow smoke in your face. Do not allow anyone to push you around or bully you. Be assertive and stand up for yourself. These people will pretend to be your friends and say that they were "just kidding." Don't believe it; they want you to fail. Do not try to explain or justify what you are doing. They don't really care anyway. There is little you can do other than stand up for yourself. But be careful – someone may try to draw you into an argument.

> The next thing you know, you'll get angry and smoke to cover up the anger.

The people who behave toward you this way are insecure within themselves and use nicotine to suppress those insecurities.

There are also those who used to smoke but don't anymore. They will tell you, "Just put the

64

cigarettes down and use willpower! I stopped ten years ago and haven't smoked since." This is not support and is of no help to a real addict. That person is talking down to you and gets a sense of superiority at your expense. You will feel weak and guilty, thinking that you should be able to quit smoking as easily as he or she did. Chances are, the person has switched addictions to another obsessive compulsive behavior.

Remember, not every person who smokes is addicted to nicotine. There is such a thing as a social smoker. This person can start and stop with ease. Do not compare yourself with the social smoker. You smoke for entirely different reasons.

As for the person who has never smoked, there is no way he or she can understand. To this person, smoking is just a bad habit. Again, your solutions are going to have to come from positive supports who are willing to listen with an open mind without the need to "fix" you.

Chapter Twelve

HOW CAN I BE MOTIVATED TO STOP SMOKING?

Developing a realistic motivation to become and remain a nonsmoker can be difficult at best. No addict wants to give up his or her drug of choice. It is normal for a person who is addicted to a drug to want to use that drug. Nicotine is a highly addictive substance, and to think that you will all of a sudden receive an overwhelming desire to stop smoking and stay stopped is not realistic.

There is one myth that has probably done the nicotine addict more harm than any other. That myth is that smoking is a bad habit, and "You must really want to stop smoking to stop smoking. If you don't stop, you really didn't want to stop in the first place." This attitude is a setup for failure.

The first withdrawal symptom you will have when you stop smoking is the craving for a cigarette. The typical thinking of an addict is, "I must not be ready to stop yet, since I want to smoke," or, "It's not in God's time." That's all the excuse the smoker needs to light back up. If you wait around for that *"desire"* to stop, the *"right time"* will never come, and you will end up dying from some smoking-related illness that with the proper help could have been prevented.

Fear will motivate you to get you started, but it will not last very long. The withdrawal, and your rationalizations, will have you back smoking again in no time.

> Pictures of dirty lungs, scare tactics, shaming and nagging are all ineffective. A person cannot be belittled or frightened into wellness.

Your motivation has to come from something more substantial. To help you develop a more realistic motivation, use the chart on page 69. In the first column, write out the consequences of smoking; put down the things that have happened to you and the things that could happen. Some of those consequences might be various cancers, loss of stamina, skin wrinkling, poor circulation, social rejection, loss of a job or promotion, loss of money, or causing a fire, just to name a few. In column two, list feelings you have about yourself as a smoker. Many people say that they feel stupid, hooked, trapped, embarrassed, ashamed, guilty, angry, frustrated, hopeless, helpless and afraid. Now, put down your assets. What are your strengths? Are you intelligent, honest, kind, caring, creative, loyal, teachable, willing, or anything else you can think of? In the last row, list the goals that you would like to achieve within your lifetime. Do you want to be healthy, live a quality life, feel good toward yourself, have honest relationships, be a nonsmoker, save money, develop a career, travel, retire, go back to school, be a positive role model, or anything else? Whatever you want for yourself, put it down.

Now, go back over your lists. Separate the first two columns from the last two. The first two do not represent who you are. They are the signs and symptoms of the illness you have. The last two columns reflect the real you. Your goals are real and achievable, and you deserve to attain them. Your addiction is going to sabotage those goals if it is not arrested. Quality living and smoking are not consistent with each other. You meet your goals by using your assets or strengths to recover from your addiction. If you're intelligent, use this asset to learn about recovery. If you're kind and caring, be kind and caring toward yourself. If you're teachable, learn new coping skills, and if your willing, put them into action.

On the next page is the Motivation Chart. Review this chart often. Nicotine addicts have built-in "forgetters." It is very easy to forget why you are doing what you are doing. Copy the chart and put it on your refrigerator door so you can see it every day, and remind yourself why you are doing what you are doing.

MOTIVATION CHART

Consequences for Smoking?	Feelings Toward Self as a Smoker?	What are your Personal Assets or Strengths?	What are Your Life Time Goals?

After filling in this chart, you might discover that smoking is a major source of low self-esteem. Most people do not like themselves as smokers. There is a contradiction between having low self-esteem as a smoker and the person you really are. Your list of assets and goals shows that you are a person with many talents, qualities and values - just the opposite of a person who doesn't seem to care. The bottom-line consequence for any addiction is low self-esteem. Therefore your motivation might be: *"I want to become a non-smoker to feel better about myself as a person, meet my lifetime goals and live a quality way of life."* This positive motivation will endure during the tough times as well as the good times when you think, "Maybe I can have just one."

Chapter Thirteen

WHAT HAPPENS IF I START SMOKING AGAIN?

Most people who try to stop smoking do not make it the first time because they do not know how to prevent relapse. This does not have to happen to you. This book will give you enough information to stop smoking and stay stopped. If you do happen to relapse, you will probably feel guilt, shame, embarrassment and anger toward yourself. Do not despair. You are not a failure. Every attempt at becoming a nonsmoker is an honest attempt at recovery.

When a person goes back to smoking, the attitude is, "I might as well buy a carton – I've failed anyway. I'm just not ready to stop yet." Don't play that mind game with yourself. Turn your attitude around; use the relapse to your advantage.

What did you learn from your relapse? Did the cigarette change anything? Is this really what you want for yourself? Just because you smoked one or two cigarettes does not mean you have to trash your whole program. Don't blow the incident out of proportion. Put the cigarettes down and call a supportive friend. Get right back into recovery.

Chances are, if you do relapse, it will be because of some emotional event. The norm is, the person perceives a threat, feels fear and becomes angry. Anger is the dominant feeling on the surface, and the person's defense mechanisms become aroused. The new nonsmoker has spent years masking anger by smoking. Now when the chips are down, the addict has few options but to become hostile and smoke to suppress the feelings.

When you crave a cigarette, think it through. Try to see beyond the temporary relief to the consequences of self-disappointment if you smoke. You have a choice: You can smoke, or you can accept the feeling, "I want to smoke," – then choose not to. The desire to smoke will pass whether you smoke or not. To be compulsive is to react to your feelings without using your intellect to make a conscious decision. It's the old "I want what I want when I want it, and I want it right now." Just because you have an emotion, you do not have to act on it. <u>You do not have to do what you want to do any more</u>.

Another danger of relapse is shame. It is not unusual for a smoker to attend a support group to stop smoking, stop, then relapse. You will feel too embarrassed to go back. You are not the first person to relapse. Go back to the group right away, even if you're still smoking. You will be accepted as you are, that's why it is called a support group.

Chapter Fourteen

TO THE "SIGNIFICANT OTHER"

If you are a person who is living with or having a relationship with another person who is trying to stop smoking, I want to thank you for taking the time to read this chapter. You are a very important person to your friend. You have a great deal of influence in the relationship. If the new nonsmoker has asked you to read this chapter, that person must care how you feel.

Most of us have good intentions. Everyone would like to see cigarette smoking go away, but it is not going to do that. It appears that the smoker should just stop smoking. After all, doesn't the smoker understand that smoking is hurting him or her? This certainly sounds reasonable, and some smokers can use this reason and stop. Then there is your partner. He or she sneaks cigarettes, smokes outside, coughs all the time and is just killing himself or herself with those damn cigarettes. "I just don't understand why you don't just quit smoking!" you think to yourself.

Your wish has come true. Your partner is reading this book and is making an attempt to stop smoking. You have probably already found out that nagging, guilt trips, manipulation, bribery and all-out hostility does not work. Try something different. Accept your partner as he or she is. This does not mean you have to accept inappropriate behavior. It means you should allow the person to be responsible for his or her own recovery. Give your partner enough space to seek his or her own solutions. Allow that person to make mistakes without criticism. What might seem reasonable and obvious to you might not actually fit your friend's situation.

For some, smoking cigarettes is a symptom of deeper underlying issues. Such people may have a very serious dependency on the drug nicotine. Some smokers can put the cigarettes down and stop, while others have a much more difficult time. There is also what is called the "real nicotine addict." This person is chemically dependent on the drug nicotine. His or her addiction is a form of mental illness. I know that this is a difficult concept to accept, but please understand that it's true. All the pressure in the world only makes things worse. The best way to help this person is to first insist that he or she recover from the affliction, and then give that person the positive, constructive support needed to recover. With this attitude, you can play a significant role in helping your friend. You are now part of your partner's solution.

Thank you, and God bless.

David C. Jones

Chapter Fifteen

HOW TO STOP SMOKING

The first thing that needs to change for the smoker to become a nonsmoker is the person's attitude toward smoking. Smoking is considered by most to be a bad habit that a person with determination and willpower can stop. Many think that if a person does not stop smoking, then that person did not want to stop in the first place. That simplistic attitude has been proven to be invalid.

Before you can solve any problem, you must first understand what the problem is.

I hope that after reading this book you come to the conclusion that smoking is not a bad habit in any sense of the word. It is a drug addiction, and an addiction is an illness.

The chapter, "What is Nicotine Addiction?" on page 12, describes how the brain becomes dysfunctional because of nicotine. That is the problem, and that leads us to the solution.

If the brain is dysfunctional, then it needs to be rehabilitated.

In other words, the new nonsmoker must learn new healthy ways to cause the release of those brain chemicals that promote the feeling of well-being. If you recognize that your smoking is an addiction, and if you then develop and maintain an ongoing program of recovery, you will stop smoking and stay stopped. Here is a list of suggestion that will help you on your road to wellness:

COMMITMENT: Make a commitment to yourself to become a nonsmoker. Be willing to go to any lengths. Statistics show that the best way to stop smoking is to completely stop the intake of nicotine. Get rid of all cigarettes, ash trays and lighters.

> The tendency will be to hold on to one or two cigarettes just in case. Don't play head games with yourself. Get rid of the cigarettes.

RECOVERY DATE: Do not stop smoking without any information or plan. That's a setup for failure. Learn as much as possible about your addiction. Develop a support system of friends, and, if possible, attend a support group.

> Plan your recovery date for a time when you will be having the least amount of outside stress.

SUPPORTS: Most smokers try to stop smoking by themselves and fail. Be willing to reach outside of yourself. Find others who have stopped smoking who will support you without being judgmental.

Avoid the person who says, "It's mind over matter. Just put them down like I did." This person does not have a clue about what you are going through and is of little help.

There is a national support group program called Nicotine Anonymous. This is a twelve-step program designed after Alcoholics Anonymous. The people who attend these meeting are very supportive and can help you get through the rough spots. Unfortunately, the meetings are rare, and the ones that do exist can be fragile. If there are no groups in your area, you can start one. See "Acknowledgements" in the front of this book for the address of Nicotine Anonymous World Services. This organization can supply you with meeting locations, literature, and information on how to start a group yourself.

Not everyone does well in a support-group setting. Try the group just the same. If it does not work out or if there are no groups nearby, you can find support from other sources. Call your local American Lung Association, Cancer Society, Heart Association, or Crisis Line for advice. You might also know friends or relatives who stopped smoking and are willing to help you. If you look hard enough, you will find the help you need.

WITHDRAWAL MANAGEMENT

The withdrawal period is when most people go back to smoking. If you do not know what to expect and have no skills to deal with withdrawal, your chances of success are minimized. The balance of this chapter has to do with specific actions you can take to withdraw from nicotine. These methods have been tested and proven to be very beneficial. Having the knowledge that what you are going through is normal under the circumstances, knowing what to do about it and knowing that the symptoms will pass, go a long way to help reduce the severity of the withdrawal. During the withdrawal period you will feel as if the discomfort will last forever. It won't. Look at the big picture. Your withdrawal is short-lived compared to the rest of your life. You <u>can</u> get through this period, and you <u>can</u> become a nonsmoker.

Nicotine withdrawal lasts about two weeks, with the most severe period occurring within the first three days.

Listed are suggestions that, if followed, will reduce the severity of your symptoms:

1. Diet: There is a direct relationship between what you eat and how you feel. The best way to reduce the severity of nicotine withdrawal is through diet.

Do not eat meat for about two weeks. This includes fish and chicken.

Meat causes nicotine to detoxify in an uncontrolled manner. A temporary vegetarian diet allows nicotine to leave the body in a slower, milder and more controlled way. This technique will cut the severity of your symptoms in half. If you go back to eating meat, do so slowly. Your body will have to re-accustom itself to digesting meat. Digesting fish and chicken will not be too difficult, but beef will slow your body's digestive system down considerably.

2. Caffeine: When you stop smoking, you could have a desire to drink more coffee or other caffeinated drinks. Caffeine is another drug, a stimulant just like nicotine.

When you stop smoking, caffeine will stay in your body twice as long as it did when you smoked.

The enzymes in the smoke cause the liver to detoxify the drug faster than normal. Without those enzymes, one cup of coffee will feel like two, two like four, and four like eight. There is nothing worse than a caffeine high. You will crave a cigarette to smooth off that high.

If you are a moderate coffee drinker, stop drinking coffee before you stop smoking. If you are a heavy user, caffeine withdrawal can be worse than nicotine withdrawal. If this is so for you, do not just stop drinking all coffee.

Instead, taper off by mixing half a cup of regular with half a cup of decaffeinated, until you can stop completely. Caffeine withdrawal lasts about three days. You might feel depressed, wired, and have headaches. The best cure is time.

The caffeine in tea is neutralized by the tannic acid in the tea. Most people can drink tea without adverse consequences, but if you are one who is affected, stop drinking tea, at least temporarily. If you decide to go back to caffeine, use it in moderation. The best thing to drink during nicotine withdrawal is water.

3. Sugar: It is not unusual to want to eat sweets when you stop smoking. Sugar is processed down to a highly concentrated chemical.

When you eat sugar, it goes into the digestive system and then into the bloodstream. The sugar travels to the brain and causes the release of the same brain chemicals as nicotine. This release gives you a temporary sense of well-being. You then "crash" off the sugar high and crave a cigarette to bring you back up.

The solution for craving sweets is to eat fruit. The fructose in fruit is a form of sugar but is not as concentrated as processed sugar. For more on sugar, see the chapter, "Will I Gain Weight if I Stop Smoking?" on page 56.

4. Alcohol: Smoking and drinking go together. Both are addictive drugs. One is an upper and the other is a downer. One drug allows you to do more of the other. The opinion is controversial, but, I strongly believe that smoking is a source of relapse to the recovering alcoholic.

> If you are trying to stop smoking, alcohol can lead you back. Alcohol is a drug that will alter your reasoning ability and lower your commitment to become a nonsmoker.

Alcohol is also a very addictive substance. If you have difficulty not drinking, you may have an alcohol problem. If you do have an alcohol problem, maintain your recovery for nicotine addiction, and get help for your drinking problem.

5. Compulsion: The best way to deal with the craving for a cigarette is to surrender to the addiction and accept the fact that you want to smoke. If you are addicted to nicotine, it is normal to want to smoke. That doesn't mean you are going to smoke, it just means that you want to. When you crave a cigarette, stop what you are doing, sit, relax, close your eyes, and get in touch with the feeling, "I want to smoke." Accept the truth and the truth will set you free. After you allow yourself to feel this reality, the desire to smoke will pass, whether you smoke or not.

> The compulsions get their strength from your fighting them, so don't fight. When you accept the problem, you open the door to the solutions.

At first this skill will be difficult, but with practice, the compulsions to smoke will get further and further apart, less and less severe, and eventually disappear completely.

6. Literature: Many people have said that reading positive literature during the early recovery from nicotine addiction reduced the severity of their withdrawal symptoms. Reread the chapters in this book that are the most encouraging for you. Look for other information on the benefits of being a nonsmoker. The American Cancer Society, Lung and Heart Associations, plus Nicotine Anonymous, have many excellent pamphlets to help you.

7. Breathing: Smokers suffer from an oxygen deficiency due to mucus lining their lungs and because of carbon monoxide in their bloodstream displacing oxygen. This condition can lead to stress and emotional anxiety. During a stressful situation the person will stop breathing, or the breathing will become irregular, worsening the problem. In early recovery, anxiety or panic attacks might occur. The best way to get through them is to stop what you're doing, relax, and take three deep breaths. When you exhale, purse your lips and push the air out. This will build up a slight back pressure in your lungs and give you an extra shot of oxygen. This is an excellent technique for dealing with stress, and for diminishing the craving to smoke.

8. Sleep: Other withdrawal symptoms of nicotine addiction are feeling tired, lethargic and very sleepy. The best way to deal with them is to simply take a nap.

Most people feel at their worst in the afternoon. If you can lie down for one or two hours, you will feel rejuvenated.

Some people might tell you that you should not sleep in the daytime because you are sleeping your feelings away. Don't worry about it. You have your whole life to deal with emotions. Right now you need to get through withdrawal without smoking.

During early recovery, you might wake up during the night craving a cigarette. You might also dream that you are smoking. This dream can seem very real. At first you will feel guilty that you failed. When you realize it was only a dream, you'll feel relieved. The dreams may persist awhile, but the sleep disturbances should go away in about ten days. As a nonsmoker, you will sleep more serenely and receive more benefit from sleeping than you ever did as a smoker. And you will not wake up with that nicotine hangover.

9. Exercise: Withdrawal symptoms are the opposite of the effect of the drug. Nicotine is a stimulant, so when you stop smoking you will feel depressed, confused, angry and might want to cry for no apparent reason. To counteract these symptoms, exercise.

A moderate exercise program is absolutely essential for recovery from nicotine addiction.

Physical activity will speed up your body and cause the release of those brain chemicals that cause you to feel good. If you can do nothing else but walk, do it. When possible, exercise in the morning and take a nap in the afternoon.

10. Stress: Smoking gives the smoker the illusion that smoking reduces stress.

> Smoking does not reduce stress. Smoking causes stress.

Withdrawal from nicotine can be stressful. However, smoking is more stressful. After a period of abstinence you will be less stressed just because you are not smoking.

> Negative stress such as smoking takes away from a person's well-being; positive stress such as exercising adds to it.

The daily rigors of working, interacting with others, paying bills, driving in traffic, and just living life, are stressful.

> If you do not have an outlet for relieving stress, stress will eventually have a negative effect on you.

Emotionally, you might feel uptight, afraid, confused, experience memory lapses, feel irritable, and just plain feel out of balance. Physically, you could experience headaches, backaches, stomach-aches and tiredness.

The solution is to develop positive stress management skills or coping skills. Develop a net-work of supportive friends, and attend a support group. Take time to have fun, go swimming, go to the movies, play cards, read. Take courses in problem-solving skills, assertiveness training, nutrition, yoga, or any other subject that interests you. Exercise regularly, work an appropriate number of hours, get enough sleep, eat the proper foods, keep a daily journal, do not abuse alcohol or other drugs. Learn to relax, meditate, or listen to music. Take care of yourself, dress nicely, practice good hygiene, and if you need to see a doctor, go to one.

When you take care of yourself and meet your needs as a person, you feel good about yourself and others. The key is positive self-esteem. Low self-esteem comes from not succeeding or from not meeting the expectations we set for ourselves. Healthy self-esteem comes from being successful at living life on life's terms, setting realistic goals, and achieving them. If you make a mistake, give yourself permission to be "human." Ask yourself, "How important is it, anyway?" You are a human being, not a human doing.

11. Communications: Smokers talk with a lit cigarette between themselves and others. That, of course, keeps people at a distance.

> Smokers express anger with a cigarette. Instead of dealing with the feeling, the smoker suppresses the emotion and "smokes at" the person he or she is angry with.

Eventually the anger builds up, and the smoker explodes in a fit of rage. This behavior can be all out of proportion to the original problem. The anger could also be diverted onto another person.

The new nonsmoker must learn new healthy communication skills to express himself or herself appropriately. Buy a book on assertiveness training. Also, self-help books on anger, fear, and grieving, and awareness type literature, can be helpful in developing healthy communication skills.

12. Spirituality: Smoking can block spiritual growth. Smokers become obsessed with being able to smoke. Without the cigarette, the smoker feels afraid and insecure. You cannot do harm to yourself by smoking and feel spiritual about it. Ask yourself

"Is my life God centered or is it cigarette centered?"

Everyone has a different idea of what spirit-duality means. For some, spirituality has to do with the quality of their relationship with themselves, with others, with their religion, or with their concept of God. I am not talking specifically about religion, although for many, that is exactly where they find their spiritual connection. Of course, that is OK.

Whatever your concept of spirituality is, build on it. Spirituality is a strength that can help you become a nonsmoker.

If you're self-consumed, always thinking of your own gratification, then your spirituality is probably negative. On the other hand, if you are honest, open, giving, trusting and considerate in your relationships with others, your spirituality is probably positive. If you are inclined to pray, do so.

Chapter Sixteen

CHECK LIST FOR RECOVERY

Here is a check list that will help you get started on your road to recovery:

- Plan your recovery date for a time when you would expect to have the least amount of stress. Develop a mind-set that you will stop using nicotine at that time.

- Find a support group, or develop a network of supportive friends. Get their telephone numbers.

- Obtain a vegetarian cookbook. Have non-meat meals planned out. Make sure your diet excludes sugar, caffeine and alcohol.

- Make arrangements to exercise. Walk, bike, swim or work out at a gym regularly.

- Plan fun activities with supportive friends.

- Read a positive affirmation each day. Write out your feelings for that day. Also, be prepared to ask the God of your understanding for help.

Chapter Seventeen

TRUE-LIFE STORIES
OF RECOVERY

Starting on the next page are 18 autobiographies from people who used to smoke and are now in recovery from their addiction. They tell what it was like as a smoker, what happened, and what it is like now as a nonsmoker. I want to thank them. They were not paid for their stories. They unselfishly took the time to share with us their experiences, strengths and hopes.

Try not to judge or compare yourself to the people in these stories. No one person's history is exactly like an other's. Instead, identify with the feelings behind what the person is saying. It is also important to keep in mind that what might not be significant to you at this time, may have a whole different meaning to you later in your recovery. Try and learn from these people's experiences.

There is one message that comes through loud and clear. Each of these people used to be obsessed with smoking. They have not had an easy time of it, but today their priorities have to do with living a quality way of life – without smoking.

SALLY K.

"Smoking became a regular part of my life."

I lit my first cigarette when I was 18 years old. A girlfriend came over to my house and brought a pack of cigarettes. We went outside so that my parents would not see us smoke. I lit up and almost choked to death. The smoke made me feel dizzy, and I started to cough.

I did not smoke on a regular basis until I left home and went out on my own. I moved to New York after graduating from high school. I decided to cultivate the fine art of smoking. It seemed very cool and chic to me. Smoking gave me "that image." I practiced and practiced until smoking became a regular part of my life.

I smoked for twenty years. As time went by, I smoked more and enjoyed it less. Cigarettes made me cough up phlegm, depleted my energy, and caused me to burn holes in my clothes. I tried quitting many times. I wasn't feeling well and was becoming increasingly aware of how dangerous and detrimental smoking was to me. But the cigarettes controlled me. I had become their slave, unable to give them up.

Some of the ways I tried to quit smoking were: acupuncture, hypnosis, lettuce cigarettes, switching brands, and using those aqua filters where you get gradually lower doses of nicotine. Unfortunately, none of these ways worked for very long. After not smoking for a short period of time, I would get upset at something, and the only thing I wanted was a cigarette. It was like an obsession. I never went anywhere without my cigarettes. As soon as I saw I was getting low, I'd run to the store and buy more, hating myself for being a weakling.

I became so addicted that I had to have a cigarette as soon as I woke up and the last thing before I went to bed. Cigarettes were always on the night stand next to me. I saw what cigarettes did to others – people who looked like walking death because they had lung cancer or emphysema. That made me nervous, so I smoked even more. I knew that the cigarettes would eventually kill me too, but I was powerless to do anything about it. I just accepted myself as a smoker and tried to get on with my life.

I finally went to another cessation program, desperately hoping that the people there could help me. Thank God, this time I stopped for good. I believe the difference was in my attitude. I also sought out a support group for additional help. Having the support and understanding from others was instrumental in helping me to not smoke anymore. At last, I'm free!

TONY L.

"Cigarettes always calmed and soothed me."

I started to smoke at the age of 14. A friend offered me a cigarette, and my mistake was in accepting it. That was the beginning of a thirty-year ordeal. At the time, it was the "in thing." Smoking was endorsed by all the famous people such as movies stars and football players. Along with being "cool," smoking also became expensive. I had to constantly replace clothing that had cigarette burns. I remember one incident when I lit up while on a date. The cigarette slipped out of my fingers and fell under my car seat. We were driving on the turnpike doing sixty, and I almost killed us both searching for it before it could catch something on fire.

After I was married and had children, my family would constantly tell me to quit smoking. We were finally finding out how dangerous my smoking was. Thank God, neither one of my sons ever took up smoking. Today I feel guilty that I had subjected them to all those years of second-hand smoke.

I recall one episode while on the job. I was in my company van. I was parked at a customer's office and had just spread open the schematics for a computer installation, when a wasp flew into my shirt. I had a cigarette in my hand, and I was trying to get the wasp before it could sting me. I ended up in my panic, burning my neck and chest, and ripping my shirt. The wasp ended up stinging me, anyway. When I went inside, they took one look at me and thought I had been in an accident. They quickly took me to the doctor's office next door. The cigarette had done more damage than the wasp!

My conscience was constantly telling me to quit smoking for my health and for my family. I tried on numerous occasions to quit; I even substituted eating Slim Jims, but to no avail. All that did was give me bad breath. Cigarettes always calmed and soothed me. There was nothing like a cigarette after a meal or with a cup of coffee. It was not until I started getting a funny feeling in my throat that I began to worry about getting cancer. That's when my conscience really kicked in.

I remember being in a customer's office when I noticed that the secretary was smoking the same brand I did. Something just clicked in my head. I told her that I was quitting, right now, for good. I took my pack of cigarettes, crushed them, and threw them into the trash can, right in front of her. I told her that if she was smart, she would quit too. That was in 1978. I have not smoked since. I realize today that quitting smoking was the smartest move I ever made.

NORMA B.

"I don't want to die the way Bob did."

I've had a desire to stop smoking for a long, long time. I've stopped for short periods, one or two months at a time. When I had quit before, cigarettes did not cost what they do today, plus I did not have the experience of watching my brother, a smoker, slowly die. He suffered with emphysema over a period of five to six years. The last three months were hard, the last weeks were terrible. I was with Bob the last ten days of his life. This once strong, good person was losing his physical functions, and trying to keep him comfortable was an impossible task. I found myself praying, "God, please take him." When Bob did die, my feeling was, "The suffering is over – thank you, God." I don't want to die the way Bob did – that's my strongest incentive for becoming a nonsmoker.

I was fourth in a family of six children, growing up in the 1930's and 40's. Our dad drank half a pint to a pint of whiskey every night. He always got up and went to work the next day. At times he was verbally abusive. He served in France during World War I and had nightmares about the war. Often we could hear him yell out during his sleep; we knew he was having a dream. Our mother was a hard-working person who felt bitter about her husband's drinking; she found little pleasure in her life.

I think that parents in those days were not aware that children had emotional needs or needed affection and praise – at least my parents weren't. Looking back, I can understand, because neither of them had their emotional needs met, either. My dad grew up without a father, and my mother was raised in a family that used children like workhorses.

I grew up in a rural area. My friends and I roamed the woods, went swimming in the creeks and ponds, and rode horses and mules when we could. We generally had fun. By the time I was 15 or 16 years old, my two older brothers and my older sister had been smoking for several years. Like so many others growing up during World War II, I thought smoking was sophisticated. I did not smoke regularly until I was 18 and had entered nurse's training. That was in 1949, when student nurses were required to live in dormitories, and the hospital had control of our lives 24 hours a day. Smoking remained a part of my life throughout my marriage, pregnancies and breast feeding four babies. The doctors at that time felt the only harm a mother's smoking had on a baby was low birth weight. My children seemed to thrive, except for frequent upper respiratory infections. My youngest son has mild brain damage that causes a seizure disorder. The doctor has never said that smoking had anything to do with his condition, but I think smoking during my pregnancy could have caused it. Sometimes I am overwhelmed with guilt.

Two of my children became smokers during their teens. Fortunately, they stopped. My husband has mild emphysema due to his smoking. He wants to stop but can't. There are stop smoking programs available, but he won't go. I might have to watch him die, just like my brother Bob. He recently retired and is going through a difficult time. His presence at home is not easy for me. I plan to move into an apartment and live alone, perhaps permanently. I've been able to not smoke for over a month now, and he hasn't. I think he resents it. In spite of it all, I am truly enjoying being nicotine free. The cravings still come once in awhile, but a good brisk walk helps make them go away. I am very grateful to finally be a nonsmoker.

KIM B.

"I have been free of nicotine for nineteen months!"

My name is Kim B., a recovering nicotine addict. I am grateful for the opportunity to share my story with you. I have been free of nicotine for nineteen months! I smoked for 25 years starting at age 16. I was extremely shy and quiet as a child. Socializing was very difficult for me, so I spent a lot of time alone. As a teenager I discovered smoking as a way to "fit in" with my peers. I also discovered smoking had a side bonus for weight control. I was immediately hooked.

As time passed, smoking became ingrained in everything I did. Whether driving, riding, sitting, standing, walking, relaxing, talking on the phone, or trying to cope with stress, I always had to have my "friend." During my twenties I never gave much thought to the toll smoking was taking on my health. I could bike, play racquetball and even run some. I did have a cough and shortness of breath but felt my health wasn't that bad. It was not until my mid-thirties that I really started to feel the effects of my smoking. My breathing became labored at the slightest exertion, my throat was always raw, and my cough was now chronic. The warning signs became too apparent too ignore any longer. I knew I had to quit.

I stopped smoking five times during the next seven years, only to end up smoking again. One time I stopped for two years. I always felt tremendous shame, guilt and a loss of self-esteem each time I started again. I would not allow others see me smoke, and I started isolating. I would not smoke in my house, so every fifteen minutes or so, I was outside smoking. Between smoking and being obsessed with stopping, I didn't have much time for experiencing life – I was just going though the motions, day to day, cigarette to cigarette. I felt like something else was controlling my life. I desperately wanted to quit again, but this time I could not find the willpower.

A friend suggested I look into a group or program. A local hospital referred me to Nicotine Anonymous. This was my first experience with a twelve-step program. At my first meeting, people were talking about powerlessness, unmanageability, living life drug-free, and surrendering. I just didn't get it at all. I had gone there to stop smoking. I kept listening for the part where they would tell me how to quit. When I was invited to share my thoughts with them, I explained I hadn't smoked for a few days, thanks to nicotine gum and a little willpower. Near the end of the meeting, someone explained that recovery is about living life free of nicotine, whether one is smoking it or chewing it. After attending several meetings, I began to understand what a powerful drug nicotine actually is, and that I was completely addicted to it. This new awareness was actually very helpful. I came to understand what I was dealing with, and that my willpower had no control here. Acknowledging the truth about my addiction was freeing for me.

Early recovery was not easy. At three months, I broke out in hives on my back, chest and arms. This lasted for about eight weeks, as my body cleansed itself of the nicotine. Also, a lot of anger came up and out. In the past, I would smoke my anger down. Now I am learning that it is all right to be angry; I just need to express it appropriately. I also found that my smoking was directly linked to my emotions. When I want a cigarette, I really want "a fix." I want the cigarette to fix my pain, anger, loneliness and all the other things in life I found uncomfortable.

Today, I have choices. I can accept that I want to smoke, and elect not to. I choose to handle my emotions and issues in healthy ways. Quitting smoking was the most wonderful gift I have ever given myself. I literally was given back my life.

FAY

"Somehow smoking made me feel like I belonged."

I started smoking in high school with my girl friends. It was the "thing to do," and it was supposed to mean you were tough. Somehow smoking made me feel like I belonged. It also made me feel grown up. I was 16, and because I knew my parents would not approve, I hid in the bathroom and smoked out the window. I would also go out of the house and sneak a cigarette. I never thought smoking would give me a problem, and if it did, surely I could handle it.

That was forty years ago. I've lost track of how many times I've tried to quit. I was never able to get past twenty-four hours except once when I was in the hospital for surgery and couldn't smoke. As soon as I was discharged, I went to a drug store and bought a pack of cigarettes. Before the day was over, I had smoked them all. I can remember going out in the middle of the night, in the snow or rain, and walk blocks just to get a pack of cigarettes. When I didn't have any money, I would smoke butts, or I'd borrow the money. I went without many things just to make sure I had enough money to smoke.

Over the years I'd tried many methods to stop smoking: hypnosis, hypnosis tapes, cutting down, willpower and self-help books, all to no avail. I would promise myself five cigarettes a day, then I'd become obsessed, counting them and watching them burn up all too quickly. I blamed myself, conditions, people, stress, bad timing, but never did I acknowledge that I was addicted to smoking. I was always looking for the easy way to stop, or a million reasons why I couldn't. The truth was, I was afraid to stop. I began to attend Nicotine Anonymous meetings. I smoked before and after the meetings. I felt ashamed, guilty and dishonest. I'm not sure of any one thing that made it happen at those meetings, but I finally came to understand that I was then and still am addicted to the drug nicotine, and that's why I smoked.

I chose the fourth of July to be my quit date. It just seemed right to pick Independence Day. With the information I had gathered from the meetings, I began my journey. I committed myself to be willing to go to any lengths to recover from this awful disease. I followed the recommendations to the letter: no meat, no alcohol, no sugar, no caffeine. I took vitamin C and B-12, did exercises, and practiced deep breathing. When I had a craving to smoke, I did not try to block it out. Instead, I acknowledged the craving and remembered that it would go away whether I smoked or not.

I had many withdrawal symptoms. My hands felt numb, I had a pain in the back of my right ear, severe headaches, constipation, diarrhea, giggling fits and all-day crying spells.

I prayed a lot and went to three Nicotine Anonymous meetings per week. I talked to anyone who would listen, and I slowly got better and better. I'm on my sixth week, and I can't believe I'm a nonsmoker yet. I go to meetings, I try to do the twelve steps of the program, and I take one day at a time. There are entire days now when I actually don't think of cigarettes or smoking. I breathe and smell better, but the best part is, I think of cigarettes less and less.

On the emotional level, I have come to understand that I used cigarettes when I was lonely, afraid, bored, angry, sad, joyful, busy, and so on. It is amazing to me that I can now feel and deal with all these moods without a cigarette. Smoking is a cunning and baffling addiction, always ready to tell me how much easier everything would be if I smoked. I thought that my cigarettes were my friends. My cigarettes turned out to be my worst enemy.

I am so grateful to Nicotine Anonymous and to all those people at the meetings who never judged, criticized or lectured me. They shared with me their own pain and success, and gave me their love. For me, that is true spirituality.

LOIS G.

"I could take cigarettes or leave them."

I experimented with smoking in high school and disliked it from the very start. My friends did not smoke, so it was not imperative for me to smoke. After I graduated from high school, I went to work in an office where several people smoked. They seemed to get a lot of pleasure from it. I guess at the time I found it necessary to follow everyone else, so I learned to smoke cigarettes. I practiced smoking and began to enjoy it; at least the first couple of puffs were pleasant. I smoked for about a year.

When I met my first husband, who was the love of my life and a nonsmoker, I stopped smoking. I was OK with that for a short time. But our friends smoked, and it didn't take long after I was married for me to feel the need to "fit in" again. So I returned to smoking. Sadly, I convinced my first husband to try smoking, and he became quite addicted. I could take cigarettes or leave them. If others smoked, I joined in. If not, I didn't miss it.

The insanity of this whole thing is why I smoked to begin with. I didn't really enjoy it. I smoked merely to "fit in." I continued smoking on and off until 1990, when I put the cigarettes down for good.

The reason I stopped was the knowledge I had received from a college course called "Life Concepts." We studied an entire chapter on the harm done to the body from smoking. I was finally convinced! The raspy voice and nagging cough that I was experiencing convinced me further to quit once and for all. I later took a speech class and had to give a persuasion speech. The topic was "Why You Should Quit Smoking." I became a reformed smoker, and to this day, I find it difficult to socialize with smokers. I get sick when I am in the presence of anyone who is smoking. I just cannot be around smoking any longer. This exercise has shown me the significance of the saying, "To thine own self be true."

If children and teenagers could only learn from my experience and not begin to smoke from the start, maybe cigarettes would be banned altogether. I suppose we all have to walk our own path in life and learn the lessons God has chosen for us. For myself, I know that I do not have to abuse my body any longer just to fit in. It feels good to be able to say that today.

SHERRY

Her life was out of control.

Both of my parents were smokers, and I was strongly opposed to their smoking for many years. Then one day, with friends from school, I smoked. If I smoked, I would be accepted. Peer pressure was my weakness. I would do just about anything to be part of my group and to be accepted. I was 17 and in my last year of high school. By the time I was 19, I was a full-blown nicotine addict. I would puff away from the time my feet hit the floor in the morning until I brushed my teeth at bedtime. Most of my friends were smokers, and no matter what, my cigarettes were always with me. It's so true: "Birds of a feather flock together."

I was very active in athletics during high school, and after graduating I found myself choosing very rebellious paths. Shortly after picking up cigarettes, I also started using alcohol. I drank with friends every weekend. My entire 20's were devoted to smoking, drinking and occasional experimenting with other drugs. My favorite places were restaurant/bar combinations. "Eat, drink and smoke your brains out" was my creed for living. Underneath my smiling exterior, I had extreme feelings of anger. I was experiencing higher highs and lower lows. By the time I was 27, I became so depressed I could barely leave my apartment.

By now my smoking was close to three packs per day. I was getting drunk almost every night and I was eating like a queen. Finally by age 33, I had an experience that would change my life forever – I was arrested for drunk driving. This incident forced me to take a long, hard look at what I was doing with my life. I was feeling very remorseful, guilty and full of shame. While I was trying to stay away from alcohol, my smoking increased to three and four packs per day. Within six months of smoking like this, I sought the services of a medical doctor to treat my ailing sinuses and throbbing headaches. When he told me the sinus condition was due to my smoking, I handed over to him a nearly full pack.

It only took a day or two before I started feeling as if a gigantic, angry beast was living inside of me. I felt angry enough to kill. I had so much rage and anger that it spewed out in all different directions. I was extremely irritable and disagreeable to all my co-workers. By the time I got home at night, I would collapse in sheer exhaustion, and start crying deep, long sobs. I craved sweets and started consuming large quantities of ice cream. I kept asking myself when this awful pain inside of me would go away. No matter how many cigarettes I smoked, or how many drinks I drank, or how much food I ate, nothing would take that deep, dark pain away. I really thought I was crazy.

Eventually, I had enough and found help from a counselor who worked with addictions and compulsive behaviors. He introduced me to the 12-Step Recovery Program of Nicotine Anonymous. I attended a few meetings and heard people talk about the many things I had been feeling and experiencing in my life. I felt like I was home. I felt like I belonged. Within a short time, I was working the 12 Steps with a sponsor who unconditionally guided me to recovery.

All of my life, I had felt like a failure. Going to meetings and not smoking or drinking was the first time I was willing to accept another way of doing things. So many people at the meetings had been living a smoke-free, alcohol-free, substance-free life for many years. I just knew, deep down inside, I could do it, too.

Step by step, day by day, I have earned eight years of freedom from the addictive claws of nicotine. I continue to support the 12-Step Program.

ZOE R.

*"I know that one cigarette would
open up a Pandora's Box."*

Everyone in my family smoked. I smoked at age 7. I was visiting my father in Michigan. The kids I played with would break off the branches of a willow tree into short pieces, the length of a cigarette, and attempt to smoke them. When I was in the fifth grade I skipped school with two of my girlfriends and bought a pack of cigarettes. We sat under a bridge and smoked almost the whole pack. Boy, did I get sick! I was 18 before I tried smoking again. I was in a car full of people on the way to work, when a girl I was sitting next to offered me a cigarette. I have since forgotten the brand, but there was something about that cigarette that enticed me to buy my first pack. How much did they cost? I think perhaps fifty cents a pack.

My dependency on smoking increased over the years. The only break I took was when I was 21 and pregnant with my daughter. The smell of cigarette smoke was nauseating, and the effect did not subside until after her birth, when I resumed smoking. Several months later, I was pregnant once again. This time the smell didn't bother me. I continued to smoke throughout the pregnancy. The difference in the appearances of my two children is worth noting. Though their birth weights were well over seven pounds, my son did not have that healthy, peaches-and-cream complexion that my first-born had. He was healthy, but his skin had a grayish pallor, and he was irritable and cranky, unlike his older sibling. They are adults today, 25 and 24 years old. She does not smoke, but he does. He also chews tobacco.

Once in my mid-30's, I was able to stop smoking for a few months with the use of acupuncture. The staples fell out of my ears, and I began to smoke again. It was quite frustrating. I hated smoking. Each time that I was able to stop, I started some sort of exercise routine. Once, I went out and purchased a $350 French racing bike and took up long-distance riding. Another time I took up running and even ran a five-mile race. Each attempt to quit was quickly ended with the lighting of just one cigarette. Just one puff, that's all it took.

In 1989, I took up scuba diving. Before starting, my doctor gave me a chest examination. He ask me to breathe deeply. I could hardly inhale a full breath of air. My diving was a challenge. I used my air up rapidly, ending my dives long before I was out of bottom time. I decided to try to stop smoking again. It was October. I aimed for New Year's Eve as a quit date. Every day, I kept in my head that December 31st was the big day. When the day came I stopped smoking. I took up lap swimming as my form of exercise. After three to four months, I began to feel healthy. My need for air lessened, and my enjoyment of diving increased.

For the next ten months, I was cigarette free. But it became increasingly difficult, because my husband continued to smoke in the house and car. I began picking up cigarettes. I'd light them, puff them, but would not inhale. I was afraid my lungs would hurt if I did. Swimming had become such a mental and physical enjoyment that I feared having to give it up if I smoked again. Then something really incredible happened. I came home from work one night and my husband announced, "Tomorrow night I'm going to be hypnotized to stop smoking!" I went with him. That was November 1990, and neither of us has had a cigarette since.

Lately, I have been under more stress than usual. Believe it or not, that insidious thought of smoking a cigarette has come back. I know that one cigarette would open up a Pandora's Box. I would end up buying a carton and have to give up swimming and diving. I might as well hook myself up to a scuba tank filled with toxins and poisonous gasses. Sometimes I have to stop and think my way through the temptation to take that first puff. For me, smoking would be lethal and deadly. This self talk works for me. I don't smoke anymore. One day at a time.

SHEILA B.

"I can't have one cigarette, not one puff."

I started smoking when I was 14 years old and continued for twenty-three years. At age 37 I was able to stop smoking, thanks to the grace of God and the fellowship of Nicotine Anonymous. Before I was granted a reprieve and given this new lease on life, my addiction caused me to suffer numerous consequences.

I had chronic bronchitis and asthma. I avoided doctors who suggested I stop smoking. I tried to find a doctor who would treat me the way I wanted. I was looking for that magical person who didn't care that I smoked three packs of cigarettes a day. I wanted a physician who wouldn't scold, lecture, admonish or advise me. I wanted someone to give me a pill that would instantly open my airways, someone who would then pat me on the head and send me on my way. I didn't think smoking was my problem. I rationalized that the reason my breathing was so labored was because I caught colds easily, had allergies and was over-tired. The cause was nothing less than my smoking!

They call it "denial." Boy, was I in it! I was dishonest with myself and others about my smoking. I minimized the effects nicotine was having on my life, lied about the number of cigarettes I smoked, blamed my job and other people. I thought I smoked because I had stress in my life. The people at Nicotine Anonymous helped me to discover that smoking was the real source of my stress.

It didn't start out that way. I started smoking as an awkward adolescent, eager to gain instant "glamour." When I picked up my first cigarette, that white roll of paper and tobacco represented instant sophistication to me. I had "come of age." It was my passage into adulthood. No longer would I be made to feel vulnerable in any situation – I could just smoke my feelings away. With cigarette in hand, I could assume any role I wanted. A favorite portrayal was one in which I adopted a posture of arrogant impatience. I would toss my hair, tilting my head, narrow my eyes, inhale deeply and dramatically and exhale my contempt, indifference, and superiority toward others. No longer did I have to appear to be the fidgety, clumsy person I felt I was.

Smoking "nicotinized" my brain. There was a time when I would have been greatly offended to be called a drug addict. Today I know that is exactly what I am. I'm addicted to the drug nicotine – a sneaky, insidious, powerful drug which releases chemicals in my brain that cause me to have a false sense of well-being. The drug tells me I need to use more of it and to keep using it to feel good, or even just to feel normal. It's a drug that demands that I surrender all my salient, God given attributes. This demon nicotine will rob me physically, mentally, and spiritually. It will attack all of my vital organs before it's done with me. Then, it will leave me for dead.

It has not been easy, but I now have one year of abstinence from nicotine. My addiction is in remission. I know that I am just one puff away from full-blown, active nicotine addiction. I can't have one cigarette, not one puff. Once the drug hits my blood stream and enters my brain, it sets up a craving which for me makes it nearly impossible to not smoke. I never want to have to go through nicotine withdrawal again. With the help of a loving God, and the support of the wonderful friends I have made in Nicotine Anonymous, I will never have to be where I was a year ago.

Despite my denial, I always knew in my gut that I was powerless over nicotine. I did not believe that it was possible for me to quit smoking. I would try any remedy for my breathing problems other than quitting smoking. I tried to cut down on the amount I smoked. I switched brands, smoked low-tar brands, switched from menthol to regular, and tried smoking a brand I didn't like, figuring I'd smoke less. You name it, I tried it. Later, when I became convinced that my problem was smoking, I tried stopping altogether. I chewed nicotine-laced gum and tried several smoking cessation programs. I also read self-help books and watched films showing lung cancer operations. The longest time I was able to put together without a cigarette was twelve days.

Finally, I tried Nicotine Anonymous. I wasn't successful at first, but the people at the meetings told me to keep coming back, even if I was still smoking. They said that my attempts to stop were practice in stopping for good. They explained to me that each time I tried to quit smoking, I was reinforcing my powerlessness over nicotine.

One morning, after a particularly restless night, I woke up, sank to my knees at the foot of my bed, and asked the God of my understanding to please give me the strength to stay away from cigarettes for good. I was sick and tired of being sick and tired. I felt a warmth envelop me and a peace descend over me. I knew that God had answered my prayer. It would not be necessary for me to ever have to smoke again.

After a month, I finished the physical detoxification. I embarked on the next exciting phase of my recovery experience, learning to feel my feelings. It's amazing how much anger, hurt and fear I had stuffed down inside myself with cigarettes. It has not been easy, learning how to identify and express true emotions for the first time. I found out that when I started smoking at age 14, I stopped maturing emotionally. I used cigarettes to camouflage emotional conflict. One day at a time, I am learning new coping skills. It's getting easier every day. It's exciting to be starting life over again.

I'm grateful for my good health. I have not had an episode of bronchitis or asthma since I quit smoking. I can walk up stairs, climb hills, run, ride a bike and dance. These activities were denied me when I was in the active stage of my nicotine addiction. I can sit for hours in a theater or class-room without having a nicotine fit. I have better concentration because I'm not constantly focusing on cigarettes. I have documented proof that my eyesight has improved. I look and feel younger and have a new confidence and self-esteem. I attend Nicotine Anonymous meetings regularly, work the twelve steps of the program, and enjoy a wealth of friendships because of the fellowship we share. I didn't think I'd ever be a nonsmoker. It's a miracle today that I am. If you're an addict, don't quit trying to stop. Don't give up before the miracle happens.

KAREN

"My gratitude is so deep I could take a bath in it."

I started smoking when I was 20 years old. I came from Germany, and after World War II I escaped from East Germany to West Germany. I remember walking down the streets of West Germany, smoking, feeling free and like a big shot. I came to the United Sates in 1971. The family I lived with did not like smoking in their house, so I smoked very little at that time. I started to drink alcohol and ultimately became an alcoholic. I drank and smoked three packs a day. I was in smoker's heaven. I never carried cigarettes with me. I kept them in my car, my desk, and the kitchen, but never in my bedroom. Every ashtray had cigarettes and a lighter next to it. In 1989 I moved out of the house I was renting and bought my own place. I was so embarrassed when I left, because when I took my pictures down, you could see how the walls had been stained yellow by the nicotine from all those years of smoking. My friends started nagging me to stop smoking. I knew deep down that I should stop and that smoking wasn't good for me, but I didn't want to let go of my "good friend."

One day someone told me about Nicotine Anonymous. On June 1, 1990, I went to my first meeting. I was full of fear. What would I do? I couldn't imagine life without cigarettes. How could I talk on the telephone, or how would my car start without me smoking? I had become sober years earlier in a twelve-step program, so maybe I could stop smoking that way, too. At the first meeting I picked up a white poker chip that represented the beginning of my recovery. By the grace of God and the people at the meetings, I have not had to smoke a cigarette since.

I did not follow all of the suggestions and consequently suffered severe withdrawal. The first two weeks were just awful. My arms felt numb, I couldn't sleep, I was restless and irritated, and I had very strong compulsions to smoke. I talked to God about them, and even blamed Him, but in a nice way. I had a dream that I was smoking, and it really upset me. I read the literature at the meetings, and after about two weeks, the compulsion to smoke left me.

At that first meeting I lost my fear of not smoking, because the other people shared their experiences, and that gave me hope. I live over twenty miles from the meetings, but I was so willing to stop smoking, that once I drove through a bad rain storm with tornadoes in it to go. I went to every meeting that was available.

My gratitude is so deep I could take a bath in it. My life today is rich, and my spirituality is free. It's such a relief not to have to smoke anymore. My clothes don't smell, the walls in my home are clean. Everyone says, "Karen, what happened, you look so good. Your skin is clear and clean." Even my car and telephone work without cigarettes. I can go to the bathroom without smoking. The first year of not smoking, I saved over a $1000. I used the money to go back and visit Europe.

It is a wonderful feeling to be smoke free. It is not easy, but if you are willing, you can stop too.

DINA B.

"When I stuck on that first patch,
I stopped smoking."

I started smoking when I was 16. My best friend used to steal cigarettes from her mother. She coaxed me into trying them. I thought it would make me look cool and grown up. She had a lot of influence on me because she was a year older than me and was my only close friend. I figured smoking was all right, since my mother smoked.

We were at a neighbor's house baby-sitting. My friend brought out a pack of cigarettes, lit one up, and told me to try it. I guess she thought I wouldn't tell on her as long as I smoked with her. I coughed on the first couple of drags, and I didn't like it. I started getting light-headed and high. That's all it took. From then on, I was a smoker.

I smoked for many years without even thinking of quitting. Throughout high school I was very athletic. I played Lassie League softball for three years. I was on the swim team for two years and received the Presidential Fitness Award every year. I played the trumpet in the school concert and marching band. None of these activities were affected by my smoking. Everyone smoked, so I thought it was all right. When I got a little older and started to get serious about men and dating, I thought twice about my smoking. Most of the guys worth having were nonsmokers. Cigarettes don't smell good and they don't taste good. So, how can I smell good or taste good if I smoke?

I tried to quit smoking many times. I tried cold turkey, and that didn't work, especially when I drank alcohol. Every time I stopped, I seemed to gain weight. I hated that. I always had an excuse to go back, if not to lose weight, at least to keep from gaining more. Quitting cold turkey made me very irritable. I'd complain about anything and everything that didn't go my way.

I heard about the gum with nicotine in it. I had to try it. It's amazing what they charge for that gum. The gum didn't last very long. I ran out of it and started to smoke again. Nothing seemed to work. I was still a smoker, only now I had to go outside the house to smoke. If I was out on a date, in a restaurant, I'd have to sneak a cigarette in the bathroom. In my opinion, this is very inconsiderate to nonsmokers. But I didn't care.

When the nicotine patch came out, I was skeptical. For about a year, I kept on smoking with the indoor abstinence routine. I finally got sick of smoking. I went to my doctor to get a prescription for the patch. He gave me some free samples to try before I filled the prescription. He wanted to be sure I could handle the side effects and maintain quitting before I spent any more money on the so-called "cure", since I was so skeptical. I tried the few free samples with complete success, so I filled the prescription. It was the most money I have ever spent on a smoking cure, but I will never regret it. When I stuck on that first patch, I stopped smoking. I had three cigarettes left; after a week, I threw them away. The side effects were minor; they hardly mattered. I had to rotate the location of the patch because it caused a mild skin irritation. The nicotine in the patch raised my blood pressure and caused me to be hyper-active, but that was about it.

I have not had a cigarette for four months, nor have I had any cravings. I am not saying that everyone who tries the patch will not have cravings after the prescription is finished. The only reason I don't have them is because I don't want them. I block them out of my mind. Whenever someone else's cigarettes bother me, I simply leave the room. I was also able to keep from gaining weight by maintaining a balanced diet and by doing plenty of exercise.

I feel good about being a nonsmoker, and I never, ever want to go back.

AL K.

"My friends smoked, and I wanted to fit in."

I was born in Sudbury, Ontario, Canada in 1929, the oldest of eight children. I grew up during the Great Depression, and we were a poor family. My father was a self-employed carpenter. He was also a smoker and an alcoholic. My mother, a nonsmoker, was a good Christian wife and mother, who took care of her family under what seemed to be impossible circumstances. At the age of 10, I experimented with smoking by rolling up news-paper with dried leaves mixed with tobacco. By the time I was 16, I dropped out of school, left home and was a full-blown nicotine addict.

I do not know why I started smoking. My friends smoked, and I wanted to fit in. My smoking progressed over the years until I was smoking two packs a day. I smoked for forty-five years trying to stop many times. Each time, I failed. I had become a slave to this addiction. I don't know how much money I spent on cigarettes and pipes, plus the cost of burned clothes, furniture, carpets, and car seats. It has to be an astronomical amount. I tried self-control by cutting down and smoking different brands. All to no avail. When I first started smoking, I had no idea I was not going to be able to stop. But now I believed I could never stop.

On June 25, 1985 I was admitted to the hospital for gallstone surgery. After reading my X-rays, the nurse told me that I had spots on my lungs. That was it! I threw away my cigarettes and lighter, and never looked back.

That was the best decision I have ever made in my life. I never want to go back to the way it used to be. Today, I have no desire to smoke. I can breathe freely and do the things I want to do. I am very grateful that I do not have to smoke anymore.

LIZ K.

"I was willing to die for my cigarettes."

When I tried my first cigarette at age 13, it was to "fit in" with my friends. My girlfriend and I would walk to the park and smoke. We bought the cigarettes with money I had stolen from my mother. When I was 17, I prided myself that I could knee paddle on my surfboard without my cigarette going out. When I was feeling unsure of myself and afraid of being ignored or rejected, cigarettes got me through. Actually, my self-esteem was in the toilet. Smoking helped me pretend to be cool, with an air of confidence and a sense of feeling secure.

I became pregnant and was married at age 19. I delivered seven months later. I smoked while pregnant and had a cigarette hanging out of my mouth while nursing. In 1969, I did not know the hazards of second-hand smoke. Eight months later I became pregnant with my second son. My first boy was asthmatic. His allergist never told me not to smoke around him. My youngest son suffered from bronchitis. He would complain about my smoking, but I ignored him. I thought he was trying to annoy me so that I would stop smoking. I did try to quit. I smoked low-tar brands, cut back, stopped smoking in the bedroom, and then smoked outside only. Nothing worked.

Smoking made me avoid love, intimacy, joy and spirituality. I was a zombie. I used smoking to relax, to stay awake at work and to think things through. I was always figuring things out, but I never actually did anything. I projected the future and dissected the past. I also had a weight problem, and I used smoking to help me diet. On some of my diets, I literally lived on cigarettes. It worked for a while, but then when my weight was where I wanted it, I didn't have the energy to do the things I liked doing. I could not run one block without giving out of air. Whenever I quit smoking, my weight would skyrocket, so I'd start smoking again. This was a vicious cycle that went around and around.

Once, After had been off cigarettes for ten months, a girlfriend who smokes came to visit. I did not let her smoke in the house, so we went out on the porch so that she could smoke. I guess her smoking started looking good to me. I was sure I could have one cigarette and control myself, so I did. I smoked the next day and the next. I watched hopelessly as I saw myself sliding back into a hole I couldn't get out of. My girl friend left and took my self-esteem with her. I was broken. I hid my smoking from my family. They had been so proud of me. I was sneaking outside to smoke. My addiction became so demanding, I could not hide it any longer. I finally told my family I smoked, just so I could smoke more often. I was back to two packs a day. I smoked everywhere – in the bathtub and in the car. I even lit up before jogging. It wasn't long before I quit exercising due to a lack of energy. I felt like such a failure. I knew something terrible would happen to me. My lungs had to be fried. I remember one day I thought, "I'm just going to have to die smoking, because I can't stop." I was willing to die for my cigarettes.

I had taken a full-time job at an insurance company. All three of us girls at the company smoked. The sales manager didn't. He was always riding us and bribing us to quit. He told us he would give us five hundred dollars if we would quit for a year. Since I was really scared anyway, I decided to give it one more try. I went to a doctor and got a prescription for nicotine gum. I chewed five pieces a day. When the physical craving started, I would pop one in my mouth. The gum soothed my raging cravings for a time. However, I was forgetting things I always knew. I was confused, irritable, and could not do my job. I talked to my boss. I told him I was afraid of being fired because of my withdrawal symptoms. He said I would not be fired but that I should go see the crisis intervention psychologist for the company. The conference would be confidential. I told the counselor I needed help, that I couldn't do it alone. He told me about

Nicotine Anonymous. I found out where a meeting was, and I went.

I had quit smoking cigarettes on December 24, 1987, but I was still chewing nicotine gum. They told me at the meeting that chewing the gum meant I was still not off the drug nicotine. I was crushed. I had been so proud of myself for not smoking and thought I deserved applause. But, somehow deep down, I knew they were right. I set a new quit date, December 31, 1987. That's when the real withdrawal began. I was a total air-head at my job. I couldn't handle the stress. All of a sudden, the manager was fired, the other girls quit and I was left holding the bag. I was in extreme withdrawal. I just couldn't take it, so I quit, too.

I went to two or three support group meetings a week, where I would eventually gain a whole new perspective on life. I cringed when someone said that after praying to God, her obsession was lifted after fifty years of smoking.

At first, I thought the people were "holy rollers." I was very belligerent and vigilant, to make sure no one pushed this "God stuff" down my throat. I was told that anything could be my High Power. The people were actually trying to help me do something I couldn't do for myself. After three months, someone in the group irritated me by being a "meeting hog." I'd show him – I'd quit coming!

At home, my emotions were out of control. I threw a telephone at my son. I got mad at everyone for everything. I was miserable, and I had a hellish existence. I decided it would be better to smoke than to be the she-devil I had become. I decided to go to one more meeting, and if I didn't get some relief, or they couldn't cure me, I was going to start smoking and never return. I told everyone how I felt. All I know is that my extreme anger and emotionalism disappeared at that meeting. I have never been angry or crazy like that since. Someone said that we get angry so that we can justify smoking.

That first year was like opening a Pandora's box. I stuffed myself with food and watched helplessly as my weight climbed to an all-time high. I decided I was not going to start smoking to control my weight. I would deal with the weight issue when I felt comfortable with my nicotine recovery. One year later, I joined Over-Eaters Anonymous. I lost the twenty-five pounds I had gained, plus ten more.

Today, I feel and look great! I can hike, run, walk, swim, and skate. What a gift! I am learning to feel the pain and the joy of living in the real world. I have also been learning honest intimacy and how to relate to people. I feel joy, love and compassion. I am free from the killing addiction I had been chained to.

I say things that help others. I can be kind and helpful, instead of being self-righteous and hurtful. Removing the mask of smoke and nicotine has shown me a whole new world of freedom and beauty. I can breathe fresh, clean air. I'm not a slave anymore. I'm free! It's a miracle!

On December 31st, 1994, it will be seven years since I had my last cigarette. If I can do it, so can you.

ELIZABETH

"Smoking was as important to me as eating."

I started smoking at the age of 15. My girlfriend and I bought a pack of cigarettes to smoke at an afternoon movie. We practiced smoking in the lady's room. We thought we looked very sophisticated, like the movie stars we saw on the screen. By the time I was in my 20's, I accepted the fact that I was a heavy smoker. Smoking was as important to me as eating. All of my friends were smokers, and I felt like I belonged to the "cool" crowd.

I had three children before I was 25 years old. I smoked through every pregnancy. My last child was born weighing only 5 lbs. Today I believe that his low birth weight was due to my smoking.

When I was in my 40's, my twin sister was diagnosed as having bone cancer. She was given only a few months to live. I moved to California to be with her. The two of us would sit and smoke most of the day. She had tried to quit many times but never could. She resigned herself to die as a smoker. When she died five months later, she was still asking for a cigarette. The doctor told me that she had lung cancer and that it had spread to her bones. I was very frightened and ashamed to be a smoker. I decided to try to quit.

I tried hypnosis, acupuncture, shock treatments, and every self-help program around. After failing at all of these, my self-esteem was at an all-time low. I despaired of ever being able to stop smoking. I had frequent colds, bronchitis, chest pains, and a cough that embarrassed me. Still I could not give up this constant companion who had been with me through all the good and bad times of my life.

Finally, I found a program that helped me to understand that I had an addiction that could not be controlled with self-discipline or willpower. Slowly a seed of hope began to grow in me. I learned how proper nutrition and exercise could help. I learned techniques to cope with my feelings instead of automatically reaching for a cigarette. When my quit day came, I was not as frightened as I'd imagined I'd be. I learned that the cravings would come periodically, but that I could allow them to just wash over me, and accept the fact that I wanted to smoke, but could choose not to. I found that the urge to smoke will pass whether I smoke or not. Surrendering my control and admitting that I was powerless over this addiction opened up the way for this miracle of recovery to take place. The shame and fear is gone. Each day, I make a new commitment to myself to not smoke, one day at a time. Now I feel free and that I am my own person.

JOHN V.

"Every time I would stop smoking
my emotions would go wacko."

I started smoking at age 12. I can remember saying to myself and others that I would never get hooked on cigarettes. It was a constant struggle not to smoke and finally at age 21, I was a pack a day, full time smoker.

I wanted to stop smoking, but I always had a reason why I could not quit. Stress at work, problems with relationships, worry about things that I had no control over, ...etc. This went on until age 54. That's 42 years of smoking. I tried to quit many times. From a few hours to as long as one year. Every time I would stop, smoking my emotions would go wacko. I could not sleep. I was irritable. I thought I would go crazy. The only relief was to smoke a cigarette. I needed help but did not know where to find it.

One day, I was talking to a friend about not being able to quit smoking. He suggested Nicotine Anonymous. I went to my first meeting 2 1/2 years ago. I have not had a cigarette since. I found the help I needed at these meetings. I learned that this was an addiction. A very powerful addiction. I learned that I needed to examine and change a lot of my thinking if I wanted to stay off of smoking. It's an inside job. It's not about will power, it's about changing my behavior, my attitude about life. I made quitting smoking my top priority. Nothing else in my life came before quitting smoking. Absolutely nothing was as important! It took me about 10 months before my emotions settled down and I lost the compulsion to smoke. It was a gradual thing.

I took a class on the twelve steps. I got a sponsor. I saw a therapist for a number of months. I got in touch with the spiritual side of me. Each day was emotionally easier. I now rarely think about smoking. My life has become peaceful. I continue to go to the support group meetings on a regular basis. For me, there is still more emotional work to do. It's an ongoing process. I now have the tools and emotional support to abstain from smoking.

This gift of not smoking is the best thing I have ever done for myself. I am very grateful for the help and support that I received from the people who attend the Nicotine Anonymous Meetings. The literature was very helpful in getting me past the compulsion to smoke. To realize that I am not alone, that it is normal to have these feelings as I go through this process of developing new ways of dealing with life's situations without smoking.

ANNETTE K.

"I know in my heart, that
I dare not pick up one cigarette."

When I was a little girl there were three things I dreamed of having: 1. Hair like Betty Grable. 2. Cleavage and 3. Smoking cigarettes. Guess what the one dream was that came true?

My thirty year love affair with cigarettes began at age nineteen. How sophisticated, beautiful and competent I felt holding that cigarette in my hand. About one year after I started smoking, a good friend informed me that I was not inhaling. With a lot of determination and dizziness, I learned how to inhale. Thus the odyssey truly began.

Over the next years, the amount I smoked slowly crept up. A lot of information about the dangers of smoking was coming out, but I puffed-puffed that away.

My first serious attempt to quit smoking was age 26. I went to a stop smoking clinic and dutifully watched the pictures of black lungs and throat cancer. I lasted about a week and said "I'll just have one." The next thing I knew, I was smoking one and a half packs a day. Again I would say "I'll have one" and that would be the end of the nonsmoking.

By now I had switched to filters as I felt they would be safer. I was smoking almost two and a half packs a day and had developed a love-hate relationship with my cigarettes. I hated myself for smoking but loved what the nicotine did for me.

As with most smokers, I justified the cost, inconvenience, holes in cloths and medical risks, etc. It is know as the big "D" denial.

When I lived in Minnesota and the price of cigarettes were sky-high, I would time my trips back from Michigan to Minnesota so I could stop at the Indian Reservation and buy $150 too $200 worth of cigarettes at a time. This was really saving money, I would tell myself. That rationalization somehow lessened the dangers of smoking.

Finally in 1987, even I couldn't deny what nicotine was doing to my body. January 21, 1987, I went to another stop smoking program. I prayed for the strength to stop six weeks before I went. That evening at 7:00 PM was my last cigarette.

For the first week, I felt dizzy, thick headed, crying and sick. All I could do was shove food in my mouth. Although I felt better for several weeks, I certainly wasn't happy. I felt depressed and sorry for myself. Why should I be so miserable and other people still smoking? One day a friend was tired of my complaining and said, "if you want to smoke so badly — do it." I flared up and said, "I don't want to smoke."

I knew in my heart that I was ready to start again. But one thing kept running through my mind, "remember, you don't want one cigarette, you want as much as you were smoking when you quit."

Someone told me about Nicotine Anonymous, and I decided to go out of desperation. It was such a relief to be with other people that were fighting nicotine addiction. People understood, I was devastated that I had lost my best friend. This so called friend was doing everything in its power to seduce me back in to its clutches. Nicotine Anonymous taught me about nicotine addiction and how to take it "one day at a time." It was only after I accepted my addiction and powerlessness could I quit smoking.

I cannot say that recovery was easy in the beginning. Every nerve in my body wanted a cigarette. All my friends including relatives smoked. I found myself distancing myself from smokers in order to survive. Gradually it became easier to live without cigarettes. The final crisis came about one and a half years after I quit smoking. My husband and I were on a trip driving through Indiana back to Florida. We stopped at a mall in the afternoon for half an hour. When we came out, we discovered our car had been stolen. What a horrendous experience!

The police took us to a hotel, and we had to rent a room until we could get a plane home. While in the drug store buying necessities, I spotted the cigarettes. I started drooling. I wanted a cigarette. I wanted to calm down and escape the ugly reality I was in. I can remember thinking, I could smoke, and I would feel better momentarily; but the car still was stolen and smoking would not return it. Then I would have to deal with the shame and guilt of relapse. By the grace of God I did not smoke and have been smoke free now for eight years.

Many of my friends cannot stop smoking. My dear mother died of emphysema and until the end never admitted smoking had anything to do with her health. Her last ten years were miserable because of the drug nicotine.

I know in my heart, that I dare not pick up one cigarette. I don't know if I have the courage to try and quit again. But today I am not smoking and by the Grace of God will be smoke free, one day at a time.

JENNIFER M.

"Quitting smoking became a priority in my life."

Three days before my 47th birthday became my quit date. Smoking became a way of life when I left home to go to college. It was a wonderful way, so I thought, to be independent for the first time in my life. As it turned out, I had never become so dependent on anything so much in my life. As a child growing up in the 50's and 60's in the rural south, smoking looked very glamorous with all the movie stars and celebrities smoking. My best friend and I stole cigarettes from her mother's purse and began our adventures in the fourth grade by hiding in the woods in front of our houses and smoking our forbidden cigarettes. Even in the beginning I hid the fact that I smoked. My older brother smoked, and I worshipped everything about him. My parents did not smoke. However, what did my parents know about anything? My father was always giving my older brother lectures on not smoking, and he let my other two brothers and me know that this was not acceptable to him. He was on the President's council for Health and Physical Fitness and part of his job first as a football coach and later as the state supervisor for physical fitness and recreation was to educate school officials on the harmful effects of smoking and alcohol.

Athletics were a way of life for me. I was on my high school basketball and track team. I never thought about smoking, other than the earlier days in the woods with my friend, until I discovered that my father was cheating on my mother with another woman. Smoking then became a way for me to deal with my father and also for every other negative emotion in my life. Usually when alone and some depressing thought would surface, a thought like insecurity or jealousy, I would in the midst of that thought reach for my cigarettes. Smoking became a way for me to deal with my problems. In place of expressing my feelings in a healthy way, I would postpone doing anything by smoking.

My sorority sisters in college taught me to blow in cigarette smoke, hold it, drink a glass of water, and then exhale. If smoke came out, that was great because it meant I was inhaling. I was on my way to becoming progressively up to a three pack a day smoker for the next 25 years. My life was centered around smoking. My children would beg me not to smoke because they could not stand the awful smell, and it made them sick. My addiction deafened me to my own children's needs. I would then hide my smoking from my children and my husband after he was able to quit. I also never smoked in front of my parents. I always hated the fact that I smoked, but I was unable to do anything about it.

Smoking became a way of dealing with my unhappy marriage. As long as I smoked, I could avoid making a decision about leaving the marriage. Only after the marriage ended, my father died, and my youngest child went to college did I finally realize that I had to get on with my life. It was a difficult decision to give up cigarettes, which had kept me from feeling any emotions for so many years. I was also very worried about gaining weight.

I had always heard that you should not try to lose weight and quit smoking at the same time. I thought "Great, now I can put off trying to quit smoking until I lose weight." Well, I just became a fat smoker. I came to realize that I must make quitting my nicotine addiction my main priority in life before anything else. I tried many ways to stop from hypnosis to patches. Nothing seem to work. I was worried that I would become one of those lonely old women sitting alone in their nicotine filled rooms smoking all day. I could picture my skin and walls of the room becoming that sickly yellow color with nicotine dripping from the ceiling. I could hear my hacking cough and see my wrinkled up skin and know my children were too ashamed and embarrassed to visit me. If I continued smoking, I would be slowing killing myself. I had thought I could smoke until the day before I got cancer.

I timed my quit day 3 days before my birthday and the day before a Nicotine Anonymous meeting. January 6, 1993 was my quit day, over 26 months now. The meetings were a safe place for me. I discovered other people smoked cigarettes for the some of the same reasons I did. I was able to express my feelings for the first time in my life. I discovered that it was okay to feel sad and other emotions. I began to feel self-worth. I no longer needed to distract myself from negative thoughts. I was able to take them head on. Stopping this addiction was they best gift I could give myself. It was not easy for me. Whenever I got an urge to smoke, I would walk around the block and yell a lot. Many times I almost gave in. Every day got a little easier and now I find myself only occasionally thinking of a cigarette and the thought usually passes. I did gain some weight in the first year. However, I have rediscovered the joys of exercising and eating good foods. I like nurturing myself and feeling good for the first time in a long time. I am in the process of starting my own business, and I feel now I have the energy and strength to handle anything. Giving up cigarettes was the biggest thing I have done in my life, and I am forever grateful to my friends at Nicotine Anonymous for giving me this freedom.

CATHERINE

"I wanted to quit smoking with all my heart."

I remember feeling light headed and dazed after smoking my first cigarette. You would think that would have turned me off, but it did just the opposite. I was thirteen years old and wanted to fit in with the older kids on my block. In our city, the kids and the block where you lived were very important. The other kids smoked, so I did too.

My home was a painful place to be. Mom was always angry. My sister and I were continually put at odds at each other. We were compared and made to feel less than the other. I think that she thought that if my sister and I were in competition with each other we would somehow be better for it. Both of us grew up thinking that we weren't good for anything.

I continued feeling that way toward myself most of my life. This self-fulfilling prophecy finally brought me to my knees as an alcoholic. That was seven years ago. Today I am sober and today I believe that I am good enough to be whoever I want to be, and I wanted to be a nonsmoker.

The past five years I had been controlling my smoking. I used patches, gum, and hypnosis. I wanted to quit smoking with all my heart. I would stop for a while, then those old tapes would play in my heard that I was not good enough or strong enough to be successful. I would give in and prove myself right.

Today, by the grace of God, Nicotine Anonymous and the Twelve Steps, I do not have to hurt myself by smoking anymore. I have tools to use, a High Power to turn to, and supports whom I can call. My new self-fulfilling prophecy is that I will be successful at staying a nonsmoker, one day at a time.

Chapter Nineteen

ONE DAY AT A TIME

Daily Affirmations and Journal for the New Nonsmoker

On the following pages are daily affirmations for the first ninety days of becoming a nonsmoker. Write in the space below the affirmations how you are doing on each day. Keep an accurate record of your feelings, experiences and thoughts. This diary-like journal will enable you to look back to see where you have been, and where you are at present in your recovery. This is an excellent form of therapy that will help you become more objective by viewing events from a healthy perspective.

These affirmations came from my own personal experiences, plus what I have learned from the hundreds of smokers I have known or worked with over the years.

"I wish you well. Be happy, and God bless."

David C. Jones

DAY ONE

Today I start a new way of life, a life without nicotine. I am afraid and I do not know what the outcome will be. I do know that I will not smoke today. My recovery is for now. I am powerless over tomorrow. I have done everything necessary so that I will be successful. I have set the groundwork for the future by being responsible for my recovery today.

This is a real opportunity for me. I will take advantage of this chance to stop smoking. I am aware that it will not be easy. I am willing to go to any lengths to not smoke for right now. I will ask my High Power to help me. I do not have to do this alone.

I feel

_____

_____

_____

_____

_____

_____

DAY TWO

I'm starting to feel anxious. I'd like to have a cigarette. I can smoke if I choose. I have a choice. The desire to smoke will pass whether I smoke or not. Just because I want to smoke does not mean I have to. Instead, I'll feel my feelings, do my breathing exercises, take a walk and call a supportive friend. I will also ask the God of my understanding to take away my cravings to smoke.

The good news is, I do have one day of not smoking. Now, I won't smoke today; and I'll have two days in. If need be, I will do this one minute at a time.

I feel

_____

_____

_____

_____

_____

_____

_____

DAY THREE

I have not smoked in three days. I feel angry and confused, and I'm spitting up mucus. I'm going through withdrawal, and I'm uncomfortable. My symptoms will not last forever; they will pass, and I will feel better. I no longer have to medicate myself with nicotine.

Even though I am miserable, I feel good about what I am doing for myself. I deserve to be a nonsmoker. I am worth the effort to take care of myself. I will call my supports, pray, and choose to not smoke today.

I feel

_____

_____

_____

_____

_____

_____

_____

_____

DAY FOUR

My withdrawal seems to be easing up. It is not as bad as I thought it would be. I still want to smoke, but not as much as I did yesterday. I could smoke, but is that really what I want for myself? I'll go to any lengths to stay a nonsmoker. I will call a friend, go to a support group meeting, and stay in touch with my High Power.

I feel
_____

_____

_____

_____

_____

_____

_____

_____

DAY FIVE

I want to smoke, but it is not as bad as I thought it would be. It's normal for me to want to smoke. If I accept the truth, "I want to smoke," the desire will pass whether I smoke or not.

I will keep my priorities in order. Nothing is more important right now than to not smoke. To help myself, I'll call a friend, go for a walk, attend a support group meeting, and talk with my High Power.

I feel
_____
_____
_____
_____
_____
_____
_____
_____

DAY SIX

My anger is at the surface. I'm angry at everything and everyone. Nicotine used to mask my emotions. Today I feel them as they are, without a cigarette to hide behind. I do not have to take my anger out on others. I will own my feelings and choose not to smoke today.

I think this is the time that I should get on my knees and ask the God of my understanding to help me stay nicotine free. My history says that I can not stop smoking with willpower. There has to be a power greater than myself that will do for me what I have not been able to do for myself. Smoking has kept me spiritually stuck: Not smoking has opened the door for my spiritual growth to move forward.

I feel

_____

_____

_____

_____

_____

_____

DAY SEVEN

I'm starting to feel a little better. My discomfort is not over, but it is subsiding. My emotions are still going up and down, but I don't have to react to them. I am in the healing process of my addiction. I'm getting to know myself for the first time, and I'm really a pretty good person. This is the best thing I can do for myself. I feel good about taking care of me. Thank you God for helping me stay smoke free one more day.

I feel

_____

_____

_____

_____

_____

_____

_____

_____

DAY EIGHT

I'm halfway through withdrawal. I need to not become over-confident. I could go back to smoking in a second – all I have to do is become complacent. I will attend my support group meetings, talk with my friends, eat right, exercise, and stay close to my High Power. It is also important that I eat the right foods, get enough sleep and take time to have fun. I choose to not smoke today.

I am starting to feel pretty good about not smoking. I wasn't that sure about quitting, but the fact is, I have not smoked in eight days. I need to take credit for my success and pat myself on the back. As long as I do not become overconfident and stop the recovery process, I'll be OK.

I feel

_____

_____

_____

_____

_____

_____

DAY NINE

I feel air-headed, confused and disconnected from reality. The nicotine is leaving my brain, and oxygen-rich blood is flooding in. I felt normal when I smoked. Now I feel abnormal. It will take time for me to adjust. I'll give time, time. Let go and let God, and I choose not to smoke today. I do not have to stop smoking forever. I just won't smoke today.

I have to keep in mind that nicotine addiction is a disease. It is not a moral issues, nor is stopping smoking about being good or strong. I need to treat my smoking with a planned recovery program. I am not a bad person trying to be good. I am a person with an illness who wants to get better.

I feel

_____

_____

_____

_____

_____

_____

_____

DAY TEN

Maybe I'm not really addicted. Maybe I can smoke just one, then stop again. Who would know the difference? Wait a minute, what am I thinking of? The addiction is lying to me. Who am I trying to kid? I don't want just one – I want a whole carton!

I need to call my supports and get in touch with my High Power – now! My addiction is always there in the background just waiting for me to drop my guard. I can't smoke just one, not even one puff.

I feel

_____

_____

_____

_____

_____

_____

_____

_____

DAY ELEVEN

Everyone should stop smoking! Don't they understand what they are doing to themselves? "Boy, am I angry!" When I'm judging others, I'm not working on me. I need to keep my focus on my own recovery. I'm powerless over what others do. I can only change myself.

This addiction is cunning and baffling. I have to always remember that I am powerless over the drug nicotine. I need all the help I can get. I need my supports, and I need my High Power to help me.

I feel

_____

_____

_____

_____

_____

_____

_____

_____

DAY TWELVE

I feel like a smoker who is not smoking! I'm not grateful! I'm angry! My recovery may not be easy, but I value myself; and it matters what I put into my body. The effort is worth the trouble. Today I have the choice to not smoke, and I feel good about that. I will read my literature and call a friend. The worst thing I can do right now is isolate. That's what I used the cigarettes for.

I feel

_____

_____

_____

_____

_____

_____

_____

_____

_____

DAY THIRTEEN

I could not have made it this far without help. I reach out to others instead of smoking. I also help others by setting a positive example. When I give of myself, I receive back tenfold; I feel good about that. I'm starting to develop good feelings about myself as a nonsmoker.

My journey as a nonsmoker is the most exciting one I have ever had. I am learning about myself. Thank you God.

I feel

_____

_____

_____

_____

_____

_____

_____

_____

DAY FOURTEEN

I can't believe it!!! I'm not smoking! I've gained a few pounds, but that's a small price to pay for saving my own life. If I eat the right foods and use my new-found energy to exercise, the weight will come off in time. Smoking will kill me long before being overweight will. I will keep my priorities in order and not smoke one day at a time.

I feel
_____

_____

_____

_____

_____

_____

_____

_____

_____

DAY FIFTEEN

I had a dream that I smoked. It was so real! Dreams are a normal part of the healing process. The addiction is trying to hold on to me. I am so grateful that it was only a dream. I like what I have and I want more of it. I never have to be a smoker again. Thank you, God.

I did not know the impact smoking had on me. It affects my sleep, feelings. attitude, stamina; it even took away from my sex life. Well, no more! I am now a nonsmoker and I intend to stay that way.

I feel

_____

_____

_____

_____

_____

_____

_____

DAY SIXTEEN

I'm starting to breathe better, and I can exercise more. As a smoker, I had no stamina. Being a nonsmoker opens the door for me to do the things I like to do. It's like having a new lease on life. I am enjoying myself again. I have the freedom to choose to not smoke today. It would be so easy for me to become complacent and think that I can have just one, then stop again. I have to recognize that is the addiction talking to me. I don't have to listen.

I feel

_____

_____

_____

_____

_____

_____

_____

_____

DAY SEVENTEEN

I have hope in today. I did not smoke yesterday, I have not smoked today. I am powerless over tomorrow. Reality is in the here and now, and I'm doing "great!" I am gaining confidence in myself as a nonsmoker. I have faith that my High Power is guiding me to my ultimate goal. The things that I am doing for myself are working. I need to keep doing them.

Now is not the time to let my guard down because I'm feeling better. This addiction is cunning and baffling. It can turn on me and bite me on the butt really quick.

I feel

_____

_____

_____

_____

_____

_____

_____

DAY EIGHTEEN

As a smoker, I was controlled by cigarettes. Today my God helps me to be spiritually centered. I am powerless over nicotine. I do not fight the addiction. I surrender my will and my life over to a power greater than myself. I have removed my ego and I've let God in. The result is – I no longer smoke. I will continue on my journey of recovery. I have value and deserve to be successful. This is the best thing I ever did for my self-esteem.

I feel

_____

_____

_____

_____

_____

_____

_____

_____

DAY NINETEEN

My friends say that my complexion is brighter. I am more sensitive to touch, smell and taste. I feel positive about what is happening to me. Smoking will kill me. I will not die from not smoking. Today I can live and strive to reach my full potential. Thank you, God,

I'm so grateful! I can also give away what I have to others. I need to be careful not to lecture or sound cocky. All I have to share is my experience, strength, and hope. I also help others by taking care of myself and setting the example.

I feel

_____

_____

_____

_____

_____

_____

_____

DAY TWENTY

I cannot believe I am not smoking. I have never gone this long without a cigarette. It is a miracle. I still want to smoke occasionally, but it's not as bad as it used to be. I no longer have to react to my feelings by smoking. I have the choice not to smoke today. Thank you God.

I must of done a lot of damage to myself after all those years that I smoked. That was then and this is now. I look forward to living a full and healthy life, without the need to use a drug. What a miracle.

I feel

_____

_____

_____

_____

_____

_____

_____

DAY TWENTY-ONE

All I wanted was to stop smoking. I'm finding that smoking was just the tip of the iceberg. I've stuffed my feelings for years with cigarettes. Now I'm willing to change and to learn new healthy coping skills to live life on life's terms. No matter what, I do not have to smoke today. My feelings will not kill me, but smoking will.

If I need to see a therapist, I will. If I need to exercise to relieve some of my emotional stress, I will. If I need to get down on my knees and ask the God of my understanding for help, I will. I am willing to go to any lengths to not smoke, one day at a time.

I feel

_____

_____

_____

_____

_____

_____

DAY TWENTY-TWO

It is important that I maintain an exercise program. I walk, bike, swim and do the things I used to plan to do, but never did. If I feel good physically, I feel good mentally and spiritually. As I grow as a person, I feel good about myself. I'm developing a healthy self-esteem. Anyone can quit smoking, but it takes a recovery program to stay quit and be happy about it. I will continue doing what works for me to stay nicotine free.

I feel

_____

_____

_____

_____

_____

_____

_____

_____

DAY TWENTY-THREE

Smokers at work are starting to get on my nerves. Some people want me to fail. I don't want to be self-righteous, but I also do not want to be abused. If I need to stand up for myself, I will. I will not allow others to sabotage my recovery. I have choices, and I choose not to be a victim. I will seek those who care about me for my support. I will not put myself in harms way nor will I set myself up to be hurt. I will use common sense and not over react to others. Thank you God. I do not have to smoke today.

I feel

_____

_____

_____

_____

_____

_____

_____

DAY TWENTY-FOUR

Is this all there is? I want things to be great all the time, right now! Nothing went right today. If things don't change, I'm going to smoke. WHOA! Am I feeling sorry for myself? I smoked for years. I'm not going to change overnight. I need to get in touch with reality and give myself time to heal.

It is so easy for me to get on my pity-pot. I forget to be grateful for the recovery I have. How I feel today will pass, and I will feel better. One thing is for sure, I have a choice. I do not have to smoke today if I choose not to.

I feel

_____

_____

_____

_____

_____

_____

_____

DAY TWENTY-FIVE

Sometimes my gratitude goes out the window. It's easy to forget how I coughed, spit up phlegm, and was embarrassed because of my smoking. A cigarette will not change anything except how I feel about myself. I choose to feel good about me today. Therefore, I will not smoke.

This is the time that I need to stop and reflect on the past. I look back over my years of smoking. Is that what I want for myself? If I do, I can go smoke right now. That's not what I want, so I have to do the things that I need to do for myself to stay in recovery. Help me God to not smoke today.

I feel

_____

_____

_____

_____

_____

_____

_____

DAY TWENTY-SIX

I need to not take myself so seriously. There's a time to have fun and relax. As a nonsmoker, I can do the things I like. I can swim, bowl, bike or go on a picnic. It's also really nice to do things with others. Especially with nonsmokers. Not smoking has opened many new doors for me. I am grateful for this second chance. I will do what is necessary and keep my priorities in order so I don't have to go back to smoking.

I feel

_____

_____

_____

_____

_____

_____

_____

_____

DAY TWENTY-SEVEN

My spiritual life is as important as my mental and physical being. How can I be mentally fit if I'm spiritually bankrupt? Recovery allows me to be spiritually whole. My life is no longer about smoking. Today it revolves around doing the things that are good for me. The heart of my recovery is my spiritual wellness. If I am spiritually centered, nothing bad can touch me. The only power that I have over nicotine comes from my High Power.

I feel

_____

_____

_____

_____

_____

_____

_____

_____

DAY TWENTY-EIGHT

For years I felt like a second-class citizen because of my smoking. Today, I feel good about myself. My solutions come from my recovery program. I feel my feelings, share them with others, attend support group meetings, and stay in close contact with the God of my understanding.

My self-esteem has never been better. I feel good about being a nonsmoker. I never, ever want to go back to sucking smoke into my lungs. Today, I want only clean fresh air inside of me.

I feel

_____

_____

_____

_____

_____

_____

_____

DAY TWENTY-NINE

My head is clearing up. The quality of my work has improved immensely. I'm so much more aware of what I'm doing, and my creative talents are coming to the surface. I'm more productive than I have ever been in my life. I did not realize how much smoking affected my thinking.

My recovery is working. I need to remember how I got this far. It is easy to forget and go back to my old ways. I will stay in contact with my supports, exercise, eat right, share my feelings and most important, stay in daily contact with the God of my understanding.

I feel

_____

_____

_____

_____

_____

_____

DAY THIRTY

Thirty days without a cigarette, but who's counting? "I am!" I'm told that this is the time my withdrawal could return. I might feel angry, confused and crave a cigarette. This will only last a short time. All I need to do is work my program, and I will be OK. This, too, shall pass.

I will not allow post-withdrawal to ruin my recovery program. I have smoked for many years, and it is not reasonable to believe that the addiction is going to disappear overnight. This period of mood swings is temporary. If I keep my priorities in order and my focus on recovery, I will be OK.

I feel

_____

_____

_____

_____

_____

_____

DAY THIRTY-ONE

My "significant other" can sure burn me up! I used to smoke at my partner when I was hurt or angry. Now, I feel the full brunt of my pain. I need to develop new communication skills and express myself appropriately. My recovery can improve the quality of my relationships.

I need to remember that I am powerless over nicotine no matter who is smoking it. I cannot make someone else stop smoking. The only thing that I can do is take care of myself. Setting the example is the best way to help others.

I feel

_____

_____

_____

_____

_____

_____

_____

DAY THIRTY-TWO

Smoking is no longer an acceptable alternative. Sure, I think of smoking from time to time. So what? I don't have to act on the thought. I accept the urge, but I choose not to smoke. The desire to smoke will pass whether I smoke or not. Today I'm in charge of what goes into my body.

I am no longer polluting other people's air. I don't feel self-conscious like I did when I smoked. I also don't have that stale smoke smell. I am very grateful to be a nonsmoker. Thank you God.

I feel

_____

_____

_____

_____

_____

_____

_____

_____

DAY THIRTY-THREE

It was much easier when I smoked. I sat back, smoked, and let someone else make decisions for me. I've never faced reality without a cigarette. Now I want to be in charge of my life. I can only do that by taking full responsibility for my recovery. I have decided that I will not smoke today.

Thirty three days with out a cigarette. I need to give myself credit for taking responsibility for myself and my addiction. I feel good toward myself. I never thought that I could stop smoking, but the fact is, I have. Thanks to the help from my supports and the God of my understanding. Thank you.

I feel

_____

_____

_____

_____

_____

_____

DAY THIRTY-FOUR

It's easy to be complacent and think that I can do this by myself. I never have. So what makes me think I can do it now? Recovery is not a matter of willpower; it's about healthy choices and life-style changes. These changes include trusting others and the God of my understanding.

I need to continue writing about my feelings everyday. Writing is good therapy and is a measure of my recovery. When I look back at what I had written and see were I was and how far I have come, it helps me see my progress. I will also take the time to share my feelings to a friend.

I feel

_____

_____

_____

_____

_____

_____

DAY THIRTY-FIVE

I've gained some weight, but I will not allow a few extra pounds to sabotage my recovery. It's my responsibility to eat the proper foods and to keep up with my exercise program. Smoking is not a good way to control weight. Eventually I'd just be a fat smoker. I will not smoke today.

I need to get on my knees daily and thank the God of my understanding for my recovery and ask that I not smoke today. Gratitude is the cornerstone of my spiritual wellness. If I am spiritually centered, I cannot be cigarette centered.

I feel

_____

_____

_____

_____

_____

_____

_____

DAY THIRTY-SIX

I am in recovery for another addiction. Both recovery programs are equally important and need to be maintained. Being a nonsmoker will enhance my other program. Recovery from my addictions is the number one priority in my life. I am of no use to myself or anyone else if I'm using any form of drug.

My feelings are on the surface. I suppressed my emotions for years by smoking so it is normal for me to feel the slightest thing. The best way for me to deal with my emotions is to feel the feeling and not react. I can use my brain to respond. What a difference, I'm now in charge of my emotions.

I feel

_____

_____

_____

_____

_____

_____

_____

DAY THIRTY-SEVEN

I have not smoked today. I am successful at recovery one day at a time. I do not have to stop forever – I just won't smoke right now. I only have control over what I do at this moment. I can't change yesterday, and I'm powerless over the future. Reality is in the now.

I am so grateful that I have choices. When I smoked, I had no choice, I had to smoke. Now if I just acknowledge and accept the compulsion, the desire to smoke will go away whether I smoke or not. There are times when I want to smoke. Thank God, I do not have to do want I want to do anymore.

I feel

_____

_____

_____

_____

_____

_____

_____

DAY THIRTY-EIGHT

I think some of the nicotine is still in my body. I smoked for years, and it stands to reason that it will take a while for all of it to work its way out. This is part of the healing process and it takes time. If I have a desire to smoke, maybe this is why. I still don't have to smoke, no matter what.

It is important to not become complacent. Just because I have a little time without a cigarette doesn't mean I can't relapse. Not following through with my recovery plans is the surest way to return to smoking. I choose to maintain my recovery plans and not smoke today.

I feel

_____

_____

_____

_____

_____

_____

DAY THIRTY-NINE

I love to go into a restaurant and ask for the ***"nonsmoking section, please."*** It feels great not to worry about whether I offend anyone with my smoking. Recovery for me means that I choose what I will do or not do. Today, I will not smoke. For this simple freedom, I am grateful.

I feel good toward myself today for being a nonsmoker. Taking care of myself is my best source of positive self-esteem. I am so grateful to my High Power for showing me the way to a new way of life. Thank you God.

I feel

_____

_____

_____

_____

_____

_____

_____

DAY FORTY

I feel better today than I have in a long time. I'm not smoking. I walk, ride my bike, eat the right foods, get enough sleep and attend my support group meetings. It's working! I can do this! I have failed so many times in the past, but not this time. "I'm doing it!!! I'm doing it!!!"

My mind is starting to clear up. I can think better and focus more than I ever have in the past. I also have so much more time now to do the things that I like to do. I will continue my success by going to my support group meetings, calling my friends and by staying in close contact with the God of my understanding.

I feel

_____

_____

_____

_____

_____

_____

DAY FORTY-ONE

I do not like changes. I no longer smoke. That's a big change. I always look at the negative side of change. I forget that sometimes change is good. Being a nonsmoker is a good change. I no longer have a nicotine hangover, and I feel so clean. I'd have to be nuts to smoke again.

It's nice to have choices. When I was a smoker, I had no choice, I had to smoke. Today, in recovery, I have the choice to smoke or not to smoke. I choose to not smoke today. For that choice alone, I am grateful.

I feel

_____

_____

_____

_____

_____

_____

_____

DAY FORTY-TWO

The quality of my life is improving. I feel better physically, mentally and spiritually. This new way of life is important to me. I will nurture and care for my miracle. I will call my supports and stay in close contact with the God of my understanding. Thank you, God.

I never realized how smoking kept me stuck emotionally. Before, when I was angry or afraid, I'd just light up and smoke my feelings away. I no longer have that shield to protect me from reality. I now feel my emotions as they really are. Sometimes it's not easy, but I feel better about myself for being able to deal with life as it is.

I feel

_____

_____

_____

_____

_____

_____

DAY FORTY-THREE

I'm not out of the woods yet. Sometimes my mind tells me I can have just one. The addiction will talk to me, but it's a liar. Nicotine is cunning and subtle. It waits until my guard is down, then my mind makes up some excuse why it's OK to smoke. "No, it's <u>not</u> OK!!!"

When things get rough, I need to talk with my supportive friends. I need to listen to what they have to say. They see me as I really am and not as I think. I also need to stay in close contact with the God of my understanding. My spiritual well-being is the foundation of my recovery.

I feel _____

_____

_____

_____

_____

_____

DAY FORTY-FOUR

I had another dream that I was smoking. I do not like those dreams. They're too real. This tells me just how addicted my brain is. It also tells me that I need to keep up with my recovery program. My best defense is to stay close to my supportive friends and the God of my understanding.

Nicotine addiction is not a moral issue nor is it a matter of being good or strong. Nicotine addiction is a disease. The best way to combat this illness is to maintain my program of recovery. If I do not, my disease will regress and I will smoke.

I feel

_____

_____ _____

_____

_____

_____

_____

_____

DAY FORTY-FIVE

I'm still having mood swings. After smoking for years, it's hard to deal with emotions drug-free. The best way for me to deal with my feelings is: 1. Identify the feeling, 2. Feel the feeling, 3. Own the emotion, 4. Respond to it appropriately, and 5. Choose not to smoke.

The benefits of not smoking far out weigh what I thought I was getting from smoking. I can breath better, I smell better, and most important I feel good toward myself for not smoking.

I feel

_____

_____

_____

_____

_____

_____

_____

_____

DAY FORTY-SIX

I am in recovery from my addiction and I give myself permission to get well. The further I get from my last cigarette, the more I progress into wellness. I have value just because I'm alive, and it's worth the time and effort to remain a non-smoker. I deserve this. I'm a good person.

I must have saved a fortune by now for not smoking. I spent thousands of dollars smoking – what a waste. I can find better use for my money today. I work too hard to have my money go up in smoke. I choose to not smoke today.

I feel

_____

_____

_____

_____

_____

_____

_____

DAY FORTY-SEVEN

I'm starting to feel emotions from past experiences. Old emotions are coming up, and it's more than I can handle. These issues have been there for years. They affect my job, relationships, self-esteem, and even my physical health. If I need to, I will get professional help.

For the true nicotine addict, smoking is a symptom of deeper underlying issues. Nicotine was like a medication. Now that I'm not smoking I need to take responsibility for my issues. No matter what, I do not have to smoke today. Thank you God.

I feel

_____

_____

_____

_____

_____

_____

DAY FORTY-EIGHT

My attitude toward my smoking has changed. I thought I just needed to stop smoking. Now I see that I need to recover from an addiction, and not smoking is just one of the things I need to do on the road to wellness. I will to go any lengths to recover and prevent relapse.

I will also keep in close daily contact with the God of my understanding. By myself I have no power over taking that next cigarette. My recovery is spiritual in nature. I will maintain the spiritual foundation of my program.

I feel

_____

_____

_____

_____

_____

_____

_____

DAY FORTY-NINE

My smobriety can be built up like a bank account. I don't have to wait until there's a problem. I will maintain my recovery program so that when problems do arise and the chips are really down, I will have a substantial account to draw on. I never have to smoke again. Thank you, God.

I give myself credit for the action I have taken to become a nonsmoker. I want a better way of life than smoking my brains out. I am willing to do the work to stay nicotine free.

I feel

_____

_____

_____

_____

_____

_____

_____

DAY FIFTY

I did not like myself as a smoker. I'm great as a nonsmoker. I appreciate myself as a living being. I am aware of my body and its value. I stopped smoking because of my health – I'm staying stopped because I feel good about me. I'm liberated. I am free to choose not to smoke today.

Other people are watching me. They see that I am not smoking, and they wonder how I did it. The best way to help others is to practice the principles of recovery. I will set the example.

I feel

_____

_____

_____

_____

_____

_____

_____

DAY FIFTY-ONE

Fifty-one days without a cigarette! Everything irritates me to no end. I thought, "If I quit smoking, I'll be just about perfect." Guess what? I'm not. The real me is emerging. Maybe I really am an angry person. Whatever happens, I don't have to smoke over it!

This is a time when I need to take a good look at my program. Have I become complacent? Am I starting to slip backwards. I need to take an honest inventory, keep my priorities in order and get on with the business of not smoking one day at a time.

I feel

_____

_____

_____

_____

_____

_____

_____

DAY FIFTY-TWO

I have abilities and talents that have been suppressed for years by smoking. Now I can reach my full potential, if my priorities are in order. Recovery comes first. I exercise, eat right, have fun, call my supportive friends, and stay in contact with the God of my understanding.

I may not be doing everything perfectly, but I'm not doing everything wrong either. I need to give myself credit for how well I am doing. I must think that I am worth something to rescue myself from this awful addiction to nicotine. I will build on my assets and correct my faults as I am able.

I feel

_____

_____

_____

_____

_____

_____

_____

DAY FIFTY-THREE

I'm like a light; the glow comes from within, but the source comes from a Power greater than me. I seek out and embrace that source to keep my light shining. I am not the Power; I am the manifestation. My light has always been there, but I only see it as a nonsmoker.

I have grown spiritually as a nonsmoker. I do not claim to completely understand this, but there is something working in my life. I will continue on this road of spiritual growth. I will try to maintain a close contact with the God of my understanding.

I feel

_____

_____

_____

_____

_____

_____

_____

DAY FIFTY-FOUR

I used to stuff my anger by smoking. I would eventually exploded in a fit of rage. Then I would feel guilty and apologize for making a fool of myself. As a nonsmoker, childish behavior is not OK. It's up to me to learn new communication skills to express myself appropriately.

My mind and mouth are starting to work in unison. If I listen to myself, and weigh what I say before I say it, I will not put my foot in my mouth as often. Good communication skills improves the quality of my relationship with others.

I feel

_____

_____

_____

_____

_____

_____

_____

DAY FIFTY-FIVE

My significant other smokes. My partner is outside smoking while I'm inside. I fear my mate will die from some smoking-related disease. I'm angry that this person doesn't value our relationship. I have no easy answers; it just hurts. It's hard, but I will not smoke over it today.

There are no easy answers for what others do. I can only take care of myself. If I try to make others stop smoking, I will fail. I could become frustrated and smoke out of anger. I must keep my focus on myself and seek support from those who do not smoke. I do not like it, but it is a reality.

I feel

_____

_____

_____

_____

_____

_____

_____

DAY FIFTY-SIX

The desire to smoke has almost faded. Occasionally I think of a cigarette, but I don't act on the thought. I accept the feeling and choose not to smoke. I have regained control over my life. I have the power to choose what I will or will not do. I choose to not smoke today.

I am powerless only over nicotine, I am not powerless over making choices that are good for me. To say that I am powerless over everything is a cop-out. I can do what I want to do, or I can choose to do the things that are good for me. Making these healthy choices is the difference between being immature and being a responsible adult. The choice is mine.

I feel

_____

_____

_____

_____

_____

DAY FIFTY-SEVEN

I do not like being around smokers. I don't like the smell, nor do I want to talk with someone who is mood-altered. I'm not being self-righteous; I'm choosing who I want in my life and who I do not want in it. I choose to associate with others who are not drug-affected.

I am developing boundaries. There are some things that I can accept, and there are other things that violate my values. The danger here is that I could become too ridged. I need to be clear about what my boundaries are. If not, others will see me as unpredictable and be afraid that they will step on my toes every time they say something. I need to know my own mind before I can expect others to.

I feel

_____

_____

_____

_____

_____

_____

DAY FIFTY-EIGHT

I never in my wildest dreams thought that I could stop smoking. It's like being born again. I have a responsibility to care for and nurture this miracle I've been given. I will not become complacent and think I can smoke just one. My gift is too valuable to throw away.

Gratitude is the spiritual foundation of my recovery program. Once I was a smoker – a slave to the drug nicotine. Now, I am a nonsmoker. I am free, no longer owned by cigarettes. I am grateful for this freedom.

I feel

_____

_____

_____

_____

_____

_____

_____

DAY FIFTY-NINE

I'm still spitting up phlegm. This must be the stuff that was way down deep in my lungs. It's good that my lungs are still cleaning themselves out. It's a sign of healing. It tells me just how much smoking damaged my body. I care too much for myself today to hurt me. Thank God I no longer smoke!

How I take care of my body is a reflection of how I feel toward myself. I will eat right, sleep an adequate number of hours, exercise, keep myself clean and most importantly, I will not smoke. When I act well toward myself, I feel good.

I feel

_____

_____

_____

_____

_____

_____

_____

DAY SIXTY

Sometimes I feel as if I have lost my best friend. Smoking comforted me when I was afraid, alone, hurt or angry. There is a deep hole where the cigarettes used to be. I will allow myself to grieve over my loss, and at the same time, I will fill that hole with a program of spiritual growth.

It is up to me to find others who are supportive of my recovery from nicotine addiction. It is up to me to maintain a conscious contact with the God of my understanding. It is up to me to learn new healthy coping skills to deal with daily issues without having to smoke. I am 100% responsible for my recovery from my addiction to nicotine.

I feel

_____

_____

_____

_____

_____

_____

DAY SIXTY-ONE

It's easy to forget my years of smoking, the problems it caused and the many attempts to stop. My program is working, and just because I don't want to smoke right now doesn't mean I should abandon my program. If it's working, I should keep it up. Right? Right!

The number one cause of relapse is to become complacent and not follow through with my recovery plans. Nicotine addiction is a disease of denial. There are times when I think that I can smoke just one cigarette and stop. That thinking is a lie. One puff could easily trigger my compulsion to smoke. The next thing I know, I'd be smoking more than ever. I will stay committed to my being a nonsmoker.

I feel

_____

_____

_____

_____

_____

DAY SIXTY-TWO

As a smoker, my mouth sometimes outran my brain. I spoke compulsively. Now my mouth and brain work more closely together. I don't have to apologize anywhere near as often as I used to. I feel good about myself and my new skills. It's great to be a nonsmoker and live drug free.

This is a good time for me to appreciate the benefits of not smoking. I feel better physically and mentally. I can breath better, and I have more stamina. I no longer smell like smoke, and I am not wasting hundreds of dollars on cigarettes. I feel spiritually centered, and I feel good toward myself.

I feel

_____

_____

_____

_____

_____

_____

DAY SIXTY-THREE

As a nonsmoker, I feel different toward myself. I feel clean, special, important, and part of the human race. I no longer have to sneak outside to smoke. I feel successful at living life on life's terms. I have my life back. I am so grateful. Thank you, God, for this miracle of life.

I want to help others stop smoking. The best way to do that is to set the example. No one likes a self-righteous ex-smoker. If I am asked a question about how I stopped, I can share my experience, strength and hope. I cannot talk another person into stopping. When I keep my focus on myself and live my recovery, I become part of the solution to others, not part of the problem.

I feel

_____

_____

_____

_____

_____

_____

DAY SIXTY-FOUR

Work did not go well today. I was angry and wanted to smoke. It's normal to be angry once in awhile – I don't have to smoke over it. Life has its ups and downs; that's reality. My supports help me stay centered and work through my emotions. I'm so grateful for this new way of life.

Sometimes I feel like I am on an emotional roller coaster. That is normal at this time. My feelings will pass. I can help them pass by allowing myself to just sit still and feel the feelings. I do not have to have my fix to make them go away. Feelings will not kill me, but cigarettes will.

I feel

_____

_____

_____

_____

_____

_____

DAY SIXTY-FIVE

My relatives don't understand why I attend support group meetings. They say, "Just don't smoke." I get frustrated trying to explain that recovery is more than "just not smoking." Maybe I don't need to explain. After all, I'm doing this for myself, not them. I only have to answer to myself.

There are people who are completely baffled by addicts. They cannot understand why an alcoholic or a nicotine addict can't just stop using. They do not have a clue. I need to be tolerant of this person. It is not necessary to explain and make others understand my addiction. It is important that I understand.

I feel

_____

_____

_____

_____

_____

_____

DAY SIXTY-SIX

I can go all day without thinking of a cigarette. I'm not cured, but I am getting better. If I have a desire to smoke, I do not deny the desire. I accept the emotion and think it through. Will smoking change anything? How will I feel after I smoke? Is that really what I want for myself? No, I think not!

I am making healthy decisions for myself. It is nice to be able to think things through. When I want something, I can ask myself, "Is this really good for me?" Today, as a responsible person I no longer have to do what I want to do. I have a choice. I can act compulsively and react to my desires, or I can make an intelligent decision based on facts.

I feel _____

_____

_____

_____

_____

DAY SIXTY-SEVEN

I used to smoke one day at a time, now I <u>don't</u> smoke – one day at a time. I can not say what will happen tomorrow, but if I am responsible for my recovery today, I will set myself up to be successful in the future. It is important that I stay centered in the here and now. I won't smoke today.

It is also important that I stay spiritually centered. My strength comes from a power greater than myself. When I forget this and start running the show by myself, my life becomes unmanageable. The next thing I know, I'll want a cigarette to fix it. I pray daily. The proof is in the pudding. I haven't smoked in sixty seven days.

I feel

_____

_____

_____

_____

_____

_____

DAY SIXTY-EIGHT

When I focus on other people's faults, I'm not working on my own. If I'm being self-centered or self-righteous, I'm part of the problem, not the solution. Everyday I will ask for the knowledge of God's will for me and for the power to carry it out. I do not think that God's will is for me to smoke.

If I sat down and figured out how much money I spent buying cigarettes, it would be in the thousands of dollars. I no long have to watch all of my money burn up. What a freedom it is to have a choice not to smoke. I am very grateful to be a nonsmoker.

I feel

_____

_____

_____

_____

_____

_____

_____

DAY SIXTY-NINE

I have a right to live and to be happy. As a nonsmoker I have the opportunity to live my life to its fullest. I need to be loved, and I need to love. I need to have a sense of value and belonging. My life today is centered around being with positive people and meeting my human needs.

I have a healthy self-esteem and image of myself as a nonsmoker. I do not have to hide to smoke. I no longer feel like a second class person. I feel good about myself. I want to continue to learn about myself, and improve the quality of my life.

I feel

_____

_____

_____

_____

_____

_____

_____

DAY SEVENTY

Is obtaining possessions and status the most important thing in my life? If I live in fear of losing them, then they control me. My number one priority has to be my spiritual wellness. If I am spiritually centered, I have all I need, and everything else will fall into place.

It can be so difficult to keep my priorities in order. Sometimes I forget what they are. As long as I take care of myself and maintain my recovery from my addiction, everything else will fall in place as it is supposed to. When my priorities are out of order, I go crazy. That's a sure trigger to smoke.

I feel

_____

_____

_____

_____

_____

_____

DAY SEVENTY-ONE

I'm starting to believe in myself. My self-esteem has soared as a nonsmoker. The benefits of not smoking far outweigh what I thought I might have been gaining from smoking. I will nurture and care for my recovery. I will call my supportive friends and stay in touch with my High Power.

It's getting to where I will go a whole day without even thinking of smoking. I never thought that day would come. The thought to smoke does come and go at times, but it is not as bad as it was in the beginning. I think I'm going to make it, as long as I don't get too cocky and think that I can get away with smoking just one cigarette. It's that first puff that sets things off. I just can't smoke, one day at a time.

I feel

_____

_____

_____

_____

_____

DAY SEVENTY-TWO

My mind has a tendency to project my fears into the future and onto others. I even act out scenarios in my mind. Of course, things never turn out the way I think they will. I need to stay grounded in today. The best way to do that is to work my program and not smoke today.

I have a God-center. I'm not sure exactly where, but when I take care of myself, I feel a spiritual connection within myself. I have a choice, I can be cigarette-centered, self-centered or God-centered. Which will it be?

I feel

_____

_____

_____

_____

_____

_____

_____

DAY SEVENTY-THREE

Not smoking is just part of my recovery. Proper nutrition, adequate sleep, exercise, healthy relationships, support groups and communicating with the God of my understanding also go into my new way of life. Recovery gives me the freedom to not smoke today.

Sometimes I get caught up in regret for past harm that I have done. I did plenty to hurt myself smoking. I think, "Why didn't I stop smoking along time ago?" The fact is I couldn't. I have done the best I know. My recovery has taken the path that it is taking. Instead of living in the past, I will stay in the present and be grateful for the recovery that I have.

I feel

_____

_____

_____

_____

_____

_____

DAY SEVENTY-FOUR

If I do not maintain my recovery, I will revert back to my old behavior. I like the way my life is unfolding, and I do not want to go backwards into sickness. The new "me" helps me remember where I came from. The best way to keep what I have is to share my experiences with the new nonsmoker.

It is important that I do not try to force my feelings about smoking onto others. No one likes a self-righteous nonsmoker. No one listens to someone who judges and criticizes. I can set the example, and answer questions when ask. If I live my recovery, others will see and will want to know how I stopped.

I feel

_____

_____

_____

_____

_____

_____

DAY SEVENTY-FIVE

I have been given the gift of life; how do I choose to spend it? Do I want to squander my life under a cloud of smoke, or do I place a higher value on myself? I want my life to reflect my gratitude for this opportunity to live and to know others. Thank you, God.

If I can step back and look at myself in an objective light, Smoking is so silly. I light this white tube filled with chemicals that will kill me. I do this numerous time a day. I even have a specific brand that I use. What's most ludicrous is, I enjoyed it. I received pleasure from poisoning myself. Thank God I've come to my senses.

I feel

_____

_____

_____

_____

_____

_____

DAY SEVENTY-SIX

Other people are asking me how I quit smoking. I tell them about my program, but they don't want to hear that. They want my "secret" – the "quick fix." They remind me of the way I used to think. I can only set the example for others, then I have to get out of the way, let go, and let God.

My life used to revolve around smoking. If I used the phone, drove my car, worked, relaxed, talked with friends, after eating and even after sex, I always had to smoke. What a freedom to not have to be dominated by that awful addiction. I am so grateful that I do not have to smoke anymore.

I feel

_____

_____

_____

_____

_____

_____

DAY SEVENTY-SEVEN

Smoking was a symptom of how I <u>felt</u> toward myself seventy-seven days ago. Not smoking is an indication of how <u>I care for myself today</u>. If I live my program, others will watch me and be encouraged by my success. My program is one of attraction, rather than promotion. I won't smoke today.

I do not have to stop smoking forever. I just don't smoke today. Reality is now. I cannot change the past nor can I predict the future. The only thing I have any control over is what I do right now. I need to stay in touch with the here and now. This is where my recovery exists.

I feel

_____

_____

_____

_____

_____

_____

DAY SEVENTY-EIGHT

As a nonsmoker, I feel emotions as they are. Feelings such as happiness, joy and pleasure can be just as unsettling as fear and anger if one is not used to them. I am like an open wound that is healing. I am getting better and learning how do deal with life's issues, problems and joys – <u>without</u> a cigarette.

It's easy to just sit back, smoke and let my life go on by without me participating. The only problem with that is, I don't like myself as a smoker. My life means more to me than to just let it go up in smoke. I want a quality life. I want to feel all of my feelings regardless of how painful they might be. I cannot be happy unless I take life as a whole, with all its pains joys and so on. I won't smoke today.

I feel

_____

_____

_____

_____

DAY SEVENTY-NINE

My addiction is cunning, baffling, and very patient. It will lay dormant for long periods, then when I become complacent, it strikes. Alone, I am defenseless against that first cigarette. My only defense is through others, and from the God of my understanding. I will not smoke today.

Sometimes it is nice to just sit and do nothing. When I allow my brain to relax, I become at peace within myself. I turn off the TV, radio and put everything away. I get in touch with my inner God. This is my spiritual center that gives me peace of mind. I am so grateful for this serenity. I would not be able to do this if I was still a smoker. Just about the time I'd relax, I'd have to light up.

I feel

_____

_____

_____

_____

_____

_____

DAY EIGHTY

I've tried so many times in the past to quit smoking. I never thought I would stop. Look at me today. Eighty days free from cigarettes – can you believe it? What a miracle this is, to regain control over your own destiny! I can live now. I have the choice to not smoke today.

Real recovery is the have freedom to choose. If I am in charge of my life and can make and act on healthy choices, I will feel confident, mature and have a healthy self-esteem. If I want this kind of a life, I will have to work for it. Nothing of value comes easy. I will not be able to react to my feelings. I will have to find a balance between emotions and intelligence. My decision will have to be based not so much on what I want, but what is good for me.

I feel

_____

_____

_____

_____

_____

DAY EIGHTY-ONE

I am willing to go to any lengths to not smoke anymore. I do not know what those lengths might be, but I have faith that if I do my part, everything will be OK. My High Power has shown me the way; it's up to me to put it into action. I am so grateful for my recovery.

There are times when I still think of smoking. I have found that if I accept the feeling that I want to smoke, the desire will pass within a few minutes. When I fight the truth and try to use will power, or deny that I want to smoke, the compulsion becomes overwhelming. When I acknowledge the truth, the truth sets me free.

I feel

_____

_____

_____

_____

_____

_____

DAY EIGHTY-TWO

When I get upset, I still want to smoke. This does not mean I have to, it just means that I want to. "So What?" I don't have to do what I want to do any more. Not all of my wants are good for me. As an adult, I have to recognize that, and make the right choices for myself.

I have to be on constant guard against relapse. I don't want to smoke right now, but that can change in an instant. Something can happen to get me upset and I could smoke again. If I keep in touch with my supports, stay close to the God of my understanding, I will be on firm ground. I can not resist that first puff on my own. I need all the help I can get. Thank God I don't have to do this alone.

I feel

_____

_____

_____

_____

_____

_____

DAY EIGHTY-THREE

Some of my benefits from becoming a non-smoker are: improved stamina, better breathing, clearer complexion, lower blood pressure, no more coughing, no more bad odor, being physically active, better sex life, more money, new friends, a healthy self-esteem, and a new sense of spirituality.

I think that it is time to be grateful for this gift of recovery. I have not been able to stop on my own. Why am I not smoking now? I believe that a power greater myself has done for me what I have not been able to do for myself. For this miracle, I am grateful.

I feel

_____

_____

_____

_____

_____

_____

DAY EIGHTY-FOUR

When I was a smoker, I had to smoke to feel comfortable. Today I no longer have to have a drug to feel good. I have healthy coping skills that allow me to make informed, intelligent and healthy decisions for my welfare. Smoking is not good for me. Therefore, I choose not to smoke.

My feelings are sometimes just below the surface. I do not like to feel bad. I want to feel good all the time. Unfortunately that is not reality. It is normal to feel bad sometimes. I do not have to smoke over it. Those feelings will pass, and I will feel better. Feelings won't kill me – cigarettes will.

I feel
_____
_____
_____
_____
_____
_____

DAY EIGHTY-FIVE

I used to think, "If you knew me, you would not like me." To experience the full pleasure of living, I will allow myself to be vulnerable and permit others to know the real me. This is risky; I could be rejected. I'll trust God that I will be received and accepted as I am.

The person who is most important to me is me. If I can accept myself as I am with all my faults, I open the door to change. I can build on my strengths and change the things I don't like as I am able. None of this can happen without acceptance.

I feel

_____

_____

_____

_____

_____

_____

_____

DAY EIGHTY-SIX

My decision to be a nonsmoker is a commitment to live. I have old unresolved issues that have plagued me for years. It's worth the pain and effort to deal with my past, because my commitment is to a quality way of life. That old baggage does not have to control me anymore.

Smoking is but a symptom of deeper underlying issues. Nicotine has helped me suppress old feelings that I have not wanted to deal with. If I am to live happy, joyous and free I will have to address the issues. If I need professional help, I will get it. I will not let cost stand in my way. To take care of my emotional needs is a good investment.

I feel

_____

_____

_____

_____

_____

_____

DAY EIGHTY-SEVEN

I need to not take myself so seriously. Taking the time to have fun and letting the child inside out to play is part of recovery. My life is not meant to be dull, boring and strenuous; it's meant to be experienced and enjoyed. I intend to enjoy my life to its fullest.

Smoking has mentally suppressed emotions that I have not wanted to feel. At the same time other emotions were also suppressed. Feelings such as happiness, joy and serenity have all been pushed down. Now, smoke free, I can feel these sensations to their fullest. This is like a natural high that I never received from smoking.

I feel

_____

_____

_____

_____

_____

_____

DAY EIGHTY-EIGHT

My life moves forward, and I continue to change. When I smoked, I resisted change. In recovery, I welcome it. I'm no longer limited by the mood-altering affects of nicotine. I can grow, give and receive, to any level I choose, as long as I maintain my recovery program.

I am responsible for everything that happens in my life. This might not sound fair, but it is true. No matter what events take place – I either play a role in making those events happen, or I am left with the responsibility of dealing with the aftermath, be it good or bad. It is up to me to resolve my conflicts. It is also up to me to accept and enjoy the good things that happen my life.

I feel

_____

_____

_____

_____

_____

_____

DAY EIGHTY-NINE

My addiction does not look like a disease, it looks like bad behavior. Today I know the truth. Smoking is not a bad habit, nor is it a moral issue. Smoking is a mental health problem. Fortunately, there is recovery. I no longer have to smoke anymore. Thank you, God.

Recovery is about living life to its fullest; to deal with living issues in healthy ways and to make positive decisions that are beneficial. Recovery is also about preventing relapse. If I make my recovery number one priority. If I meet my responsibility to myself, everything will fall into place as it is supposed to.

I feel

_____

_____

_____

_____

_____

_____

DAY NINETY

Ninety days without a cigarette and I'm not a basket case!! Today I'm a problem solver, not a problem maker. I feel good about myself as a non-smoker. This is a blinding-light miracle! I have achieved my goal! I am a recovering nicotine addict! Thank you, God!

New doors can open up for me. I can go where I please, be with whom ever I want and not have to worry about how I can smoke or how I smell. What a freedom it is to no long be a slave to my addiction to nicotine. I know that I will never be cured from the addiction, but I do not have to smoke anymore.

I feel
_____

_____

_____

_____

_____

_____

_____